Life of Pie
Nag Pie
(Fifty More Shades of Nagging)

Chris Gibson

alliebooks

Published by alliebooks.co.uk

Life of Pie
Nag Pie!
Fifty More Shades of Nagging
By Chris Gibson

Published by:
alliebooks.co.uk
A Division of Franology Limited
9 Catherines Close
Solihull
West Midlands
B91 2SZ

Parent: 978-1-909429-06-2
ePub version: 978-1-909429-07-9
Mobi version: 978-1-909429-08-6

Copyright © 2013 Chris Gibson
orders@alliebooks.co.uk
www.alliebooks.co.uk

alliebooks

ORIGINAL eBOOKS

ePublished by Original eBooks
a division of Original Writing (UK) Limited - an Original Writing Group company

This book is intended as a light-hearted observation of relationships only, not as a definitive scientific manual. The opinions of the author are intended as a monologue and are in no way intended to offend anyone. Any reference to an experience is not directed at any one individual and any reference to an individual by name, implied in the narrative or any association is purely coincidental. The author does not accept any liability in the event that any individual assumes that any reference may be based on that individual.

Should any individual consider any of the narrative is directed at them then the author would like to suggest that they shouldn't flatter themselves!

Preface

In Fifty Shades of Nagging we looked at some of those wonderful clichés, comments and statements of intent that our partners use every day. It was received to critical acclaim and although not a true parody in the sense of an alternative erotic novel, the narrative was such that it was more anecdotal despite the category it ended up in on eBook charts!

Here we are again with Fifty Shades More, this time a journey through life, a Life of Pie – Nag Pie and the various stages of nagging from daughters, little women, fiancés, wives, before and after divorce and into the silver surfer time of life. The phases and stages of a woman's life are a never ending saga of baking and passing on slices of that 'nag pie' to grandchildren, grown up sons and to husbands that have avoided the unfortunate divorce and remained in a loving but nagging environment!

As one review said, of Fifty Shades of Nagging, "like all men who venture any generalized criticism of women - he will get slated as a misogynist. This is a shame as there are some positive things about men that women could actually learn from this book." Misogynist? Never, the author loves women not hates them! Therefore in an attempt to offer a balanced view this second book has a sprinkling of counter opinion and observation, just for kicks, and to placate the misandrist's!

Whether you are a man, a woman or someone in a same sex partnership this second offering should raise a smile, cause a debate or lead to more nagging for agreeing with the next Fifty or so Shades of Nagging – a Life of Pie - Nag Pie ... good luck!

Contents

About the Author

Chris Gibson is an author and co-author of many serious, well fairly serious, business books and spends the rest of his life actually trying to make a living by working in the franchise industry, whatever that means.

Anyway, this second offering will probably alienate even more women, some even clients, despite the fact that it is more tongue in cheek nonsense!

Still a devoted father, even though his daughter is now a teenager, this minor hiccup has not stopped him trying to enjoy life and attempt to dodge 'nagging' from all directions.

This second book written about 'Nagging' is further light-hearted observation gleaned from years of first hand experience and indeed a few stories shared with friends, especially after publication of Fifty Shades of Nagging. More impressive is that some of these stories have come from women, eager to share the details, perhaps in the hope that they can claim ownership if contained in this offering.

Follow on Twitter @ChrisGAuthor
Facebook – Chris Gibson Author Page

Acknowledgments

To my daughter Allie, clearly the reference to daughters herein has nothing to do with you; in my eyes you are perfect!

To my mother, who continues to worry about everything I do and everything I buy!

To Don, my brother, for laughing out loud and the ever present encouragement

In memory of Dad, if you were here I know you would have provided a story or two, as you're not this is for you.

To my estranged wife Helen, this one isn't about you either! But thanks for the support and a hint of material – from your own observations of others of course!

To the ladies that now approach me with caution, just in case I include an anecdote about them in this book. To those ladies that have offered a story or two, I thank you even more.

To the men and women of the world – nothing has changed since the first book so it stands a chance that nothing will change...
ever!

1

Here We Are Again!

Fallout!

Well here we are again, the second offering and a sequel, to Fifty Shades of Nagging – Most of Them Grey! Hopefully this collection of another fifty or so examples will follow the success of the first one!

I say success loosely, the 'so called' success is in the number of downloads and copies sold, which is very nice thank you, but the real success is my delight in how women now speak to me, with some caution just in case I analyse it an fire a flippant comment back... result!

They say with success comes a level of sacrifice, and although this newfound caution shown by some women towards me is delightful, the downside is grief from those convinced that I have given the closely guarded secrets away to the world about how women think. For those ladies who thought that I deserved a big slice of 'nag pie' for having the audacity to commit women's secrets to text, you will be pleased that I did get lots of grief and from ex's, my mother and plenty of female acquaintances for being a chauvinistic pig, well one or ten said to me! I think it was a bit of 'nagging', but I couldn't possibly comment with any conviction! In this sequel I have pondered how the heck I can write another fifty or so phrases, comments, and actions that again all add up to what men often call 'nagging', but after a few seconds it became abundantly clear that there was plenty more material to include in this sequel, it is after all a never ending saga, as someone commented on my Facebook Author Page!

To be honest men will always take criticism as 'nagging' and so the material for this and subsequent books is always going to be in abundance. Men will always switch off and close their minds even if the comments are right and maybe, just maybe justified. While on the subject of closing one's mind the next reference to a certain song by Alexander O'Neal will let the women of the world know what men are prob-ably thinking; and so to the immortal words of Alex;

"Can't you find something else to talk about? Is this song the only song you sing? Makes you look better when you put me down, value your opinion. Don't criticize my friends, criticize my ideals, don't criticize my lifestyle, I'm fed up cause all you want to do is criticize."

Songs and lyrics, they connect to us in different ways and we will look at some more a bit later in the book, appropriate ones that can be used as ringtones for certain people. Here I go again, finger on the misogy-nist button ready to launch a barrage of abuse in the general direction of women, some would say. This is certainly not the intention as I actually love women, love what they say and the recommendations I have been privy to in the last forty or so years. How did that sound? Genuine, oh good I am pleased.

What else is in the book? Well by popular demand, more comments that older ladies say and while run-ning the risk of being disinherited for sharing a few more comments from my mother's mouth, the oppor-tunity to share with you is too much to resist, so there are more to follow in subsequent chapters. It was a tough decision, actually no it wasn't really especially when I saw the tears running down my brothers face when he was reading the last book, so if anything this book is for him...just remember though Don, if I am disinherited you can share! Still, knowing our luck the government will change the inheritance tax thresholds and there will be nothing left anyway; especially if the nursing home care takes the lion's share! All those years of 'nagging' and no pay out, brilliant!

Other bits of fallout, you will be delighted to read, include women that now look at me in a really funny way, as if I have a little goatee beard, bow tie, notepad and round glasses. All of a sudden I am seen as a psychologist with an east European accent, strumming an imaginary beard and analysing what they say. It's bloody hilarious in truth, I can now see the cogs working inside some women's heads, unsure whether to say anything critical to me for fear that it might appear in this second book. I think I have cracked it! Who am I fooling; utter twaddle Gibson, there is never a chance of that happening.

Okay, shall we get something straight here? Despite the erroneous assumption from a few people, I am not a qualified psychologist or indeed any other medical 'ologist', just a bloke, a philosopher that has an opinion or two and sees the funny side of 'nagging'. But let us also remember that Sigmund Freud, Alfred Adler and even John Dewey had their own dissenters and much of their opinion was labelled as extreme, so perhaps this drivel will fall into the same category one day. The intention is to explore the funny side of the communication breakdown and although there is a smidgen of psychobabble mixed in, that you could read as analysis, it certainly isn't intended as another dissertation or thesis. Let us face it if it was it would need far more research and quite honestly 47 years is more than enough thank you. Of course if any top university would like to adopt the theory and award a doctorate, I do enjoy a good old-fashioned graduation gown ceremony, so give me a call.

Of course this opening page or two assumes that you have read the first book, but don't despair if you didn't it isn't like the Star Wars films. This isn't the second in the series, Episode V, but to understand you needed to see Episode IV first. Or indeed have to piece together the prequels I, II and III, produced by George Lucas after Episode VI! Are you with me? Hope so, but of course if you do want to buy the first book my very patient and helpful bank manager would be delighted! This is therefore a collection of another batch of observations put into another eight chapters under subject titles that reflect the journey through life, a 'Life of Nagging', indeed a 'Life of Pie – Nag Pie.' So with all this planning I suppose this is a structured sequel; jeez whatever next a defined and logical analysis of 'nagging', never in a million years.

You can read it from a man's perspective or from a woman's, but I thought it might be a good idea to take you through the phases of life, hence the title, a 'Life of Pie' whereby a man receives a slice of 'nag pie' from females of every age; starting with daughters, moving on to 'little women' who in turn get engaged and plan their wedding and then continue to bake new pies during family life adorning the table with different pies at social gatherings causing havoc. We will share those unfortunate comments that make a mockery of balance in any relationship and move onto some of the crazy comments that can bring on separation and eventually divorce. Don't panic this isn't a Tim Burton approach to the book i.e. a bit dark and disturbing, but even more of a satirical look at what is said and more importantly how it is said. By the way 'nagging' doesn't stop with a 'decree absolute' either, it unfortunately continues for many estranged partners, who believe that despite parting company they still have the right to 'av a go' for old times sake! Probably justification for the decision made to walk away and jump over the fence to the green side, which turned out to be concrete in the end. Concrete that a man laid, most likely, and painted green with a can of Leyland heavy-duty floor paint.

For those couples who work at the relationship and continue onward and downward, the 'silver surf nagging' phase in a "Life of Pie' often bring out the best cutting comments...ever! Men grow thicker skin and just take the punishment, which in turn simply increases the intensity of the 'nagging'. Bless them!

I have also listened to my female public, yes all of you, that have made suggestions in Amazon Reviews and on Twitter and Facebook that it would be nice to have the book written from a female perspective. Of course no lady, to my knowledge, has offered a new manuscript as yet to a publisher, and so that leaves me with a couple of choices. First I could adopt a pen name like Christine Gibson, or maybe use one of the ex wives names, and write a different book aimed at blokes... tempting. The second choice is to throw a chapter in at the end of here with self-criticism and a showing of my female side.... yes, that works and so that is what I decided to do. The last chapter was nearly called Fifty Shades of Bragging as it covered some of the garbage that men come out with, verbal garbage if not even verbal diarrhea. Thanks Claire, for the idea, even though the suggestion was for a whole book about our idiosyncrasies that you were asking for.

Although this concession is made to improve the book, I have however ignored the one comment made on what a waste of money the first book was, with no constructive critique, safe in the knowledge that the author of that comment is unlikely to be reading this follow up.

The first book looked at words, shopping, work, and the brilliant cross-examination techniques, DIY and then the last word. Now there might be some cross-over here with additional comments in the long journey we are about to undertake in the lifelong expedition. However if there are any unintentional but perceived replications they are intended to reinforce the male categorisation that criticism is just plain 'nagging', albeit in a slightly more descriptive way. This book is longer than Fifty Shades of Nagging, which was originally only written as a pure eBook, but quickly became an 'in demand' paperback too. This one is a bit more analysis and more anecdotes with a sprinkle of psychology on top.

To start, here's the appetiser, a warm up to the main content but none the less a selection of some more of those words that leave men wondering.

More Words to Ponder

Where to continue this time? More words, those single little beauties that can spark fear into a man, a sense of foreboding, lack of emotional control or worse lack of control of bodily functions!

How we interpret these words is the humorous side to what are often said without any agenda by a woman or partner. Agenda or not they deserve a mention to set the tone for the rest of the book. These words are often a prelude to the main performance, the really juicy criticism bit, the really painful bit and the really hard-core slice to the guts bit. Which is a great way to start... 'Really' it is.

Really: (adjective) 1. You now have three seconds to change what you just said. 2. The lull before the storm. 3. Confirmation of a lie, noted and to be used in evidence. 4. An exclamation of disbelief.

If you are sparring with words it's a feint, a jab. It can put you off your guard right before the pending verbal right hook.

Think of the times when a bloke has spewed a purely logical answer to a question all over the floor, one that he completely believes in and one word is said, "Really". Immediately a man reverts to his very short-term memory and retraces each word said, inserting punctuation and repeating it in his head again, wondering if it was a feasible answer. Is it hell, there must be a flaw in the comment he has just made, maybe the punctuation was out of sync and it came across all wrong. Is it time to quickly read 'Eats, Shoots and Leaves'...or is it 'Eats Shoots and Leaves' you know, that brilliant book on punctuation that lives in the bookcase? NO TIME, bugger it!

The trouble with 'Really' is that it is nondescript; it gives men absolutely no clue on what a woman is thinking...that's why it's a blinder for women to play! It can be used in almost any conversation; even discussions that are going well and really is dropped in from nowhere. Gotta love it 'really'!

Charming: (noun) 1. You pig! 2. I didn't like that, but can't think of a quick 'nag' so this will fill the gap. 3. Okay getting personal, right gloves are off then.

We have all heard it or said it and if you add a few

letters and take a few away 'Charming' can be quickly translated into 'B****rd!'

It usually comes into the dialogue right after a bloke has had enough of the 'nagging' and in an attempt to get 'one up' in the points tally a little personal dig is used. Something about weight gain, sagging parts, loss of sparkle not only in a woman's eyes with added crows feet, but under the duvet maybe...blah blah blah.

Now, if a man steeps to this level then he should really expect 'Charming' probably followed up with what can be called a 'mirror insult', an insult that goes a bit further, such as his tummy fat, his shrinking parts and lack of rigidity in the once 'rock hard' region...stooping lower. It might escalate from a lack of rigidity to the lack of feeling at all! Flaccid is a terrible word after all, and even worse 'erectile dysfunction' can hurt a bloke, even with no feeling down there. So I am led to believe!

Of course the conversation might have been totally innocent and without any reference to gravitational effect on various parts of the body or the effect that her weight has on the tidal flow to say, the Atlantic Ocean. A lot of the time it's a misunderstanding from what was said before. Honestly, just a misunderstanding!

Disinterest in the conversation and not paying attention to every word can result in 'Charming' for not doting on her every word! "You just don't listen, do you." Well actually no, we don't and for all females here is a little known male attribute... we all have a little knob, no not that one, a little knob that we turn like a radio dial to tune in and out on demand; it is a great tool, a useful tool and a tool that only a man can work properly. So 'men of the world' pay homage and say out loud ..."all hail the little knob."

Nice: (verb) 1. A 'Full Stop.' 2. It's shite really. 3. Is that your way of apologising? 4. How do I say this without offending you...oh well I don't

Nice is like 'fine', in fact its four letters too and includes the same two vowels with a couple of consonant changes, so it stands a chance that it first came from the same alternative dictionary of 'nagging' words.

How this word is said has different meanings, when said with a smile and a higher pitch it really is 'nice' the air is fresh the sun is out and a man has nothing to worry about...yet! When it is said with a straight face and uttered quickly it is another kettle of fish. It reeks of ire, sarcasm and will definitely lead to something far darker.

But by far the worst way a man can hear 'nice' is when it is combined with vacant eyes or worse said while avoiding eye contact and looking instead at your left testicle and uttered in a pretty non committal way. Why is this worse? Because it leaves a man in limbo, is it good or is it bad?...crap you can't tell... argh!

What to do, what to do?... Try and make it better?... Say something or shut up? While pondering the best choice, men break out in a cold sweat as they try to decipher whether it is the pleasant 'nice' or the damming 'nice'.

Take solace 'men of the world' that this mid range 'nice' is more than likely the one that means you have committed a howler. 'Nice' in response to the present from La Senza, she is a size 10 not a 14 you clump nugget! Daffodils are 'nice' but she prefers Lilies, you know that. Or even the steak house is 'nice' to eat out in but the local Italian eatery is far classier and "so what if it's twice the price."

Occasionally making the effort and being spontaneous brings out the non-committal 'nice' comment. Men really don't like this form of 'nice' and in their attempt to hear 'fantastic' or 'wonderful' they try and put a little effort in. Unfortunately this exercise can lead to a howler too.

For example, picture a couple discussing the home finances and for those few minutes reality kicks in and THEY decide that going out every Friday for something to eat is a waste of money with the credit cards maxed out from shopping sprees. (see the first book!) A candid discussion ensues and joint agreement made...is it heck! Friday night rolls around and in an attempt to make the grown up time a little bit more special our man walks in with a meal for two from M&S, including wine and desert for a tenner. Good deed for the day done, a levelheaded, a very thoughtful approach and with a pinch of spontaneity, he is convinced that he has done the right thing with his special thought. Actually no!

Instead he is greeted by a recently showered woman dressed in a little black dress, with some of those big pants underneath to flatten the bulge, and a full face of makeup troweled on with a real effort clearly made on the Touché éclat concealer around the eyes. For a second he considers a quick nervous gag about the 'paint by numbers approach' but errs on the side of caution. What comes out of his mouth is never going to be right is it? Even "you look 'nice' for a 'nice' night in."

He is greeted with a blank look, and in a nanosecond it is clear that the joint agreement to stay in, made last week, was not 'really' meant. Has he missed a hint during a conversation about something or other? Or is it that he completely misunderstood the discussion and the translation of 'staying in' actually meant 'take me out'. "Nice!" she says, which puts him on the back foot again, is it what he just said about her looking 'nice' or is it because she is racked off because his idea of a romantic night in at little cost is a crap spontaneous idea? Either way the immortal word 'nice' has put him in the doghouse; roll on the next slice of 'nag pie.' Is it too late to take the M&S meal back, he wonders!

I could go on for pages and pages about more of these little gems, but in the interests of keeping on track with the main content of the book let us move on to the stages of evolution for a woman and her ever developing special skill of short sharp 'nagging' and keeping men in line, a 'Life of Pie – Nag Pie!'

Instead of starting a new Chapter here, I have wimped out and kept the reference to daughters in this the introduction to the book, hopefully the fact that it is lost in the contents page and not as a separate Chapter item, this clever omission will save me from more fallout from the offspring! I can live in hope but deep down I know that she will probably read this and so Allie, this next bit is nothing to do with you at all. It is what other fathers have told me, and no you can't have an iMac unless this becomes a best seller!

Daughters Nag Dad's

Under the tuition of mothers, sisters, perhaps even great aunts and grandmothers, who are all fifth degree black belts in the martial art of 'nagging', daughters learn to have their say from an early age.

Some daughters are worse than others, especially if mum is a dab hand at the fine art of 'nagging'. Nurture of a little girl through home schooling can accelerate the learning process. Even if that very strong and special relationship between fathers and daughters holds firm it is clear that the occasional comment is reminiscent of a conversation between daddy and mummy.

Hormones kicking in of course contribute to the teenage years and the urge to take frustration out on daddy, but any dad that hides behind that excuse faces the wrath of their offspring if suggested as a logical excuse to the mood swing. Indeed it will have the same reaction experienced with a woman when unwittingly a certain time of the month is suggested as a reason for the overreaction. How often have men wished they hadn't referred to the pending monthly visit from the painters and decorators? ...Dangerous ground!

Don't forget that adolescence is a 'proving ground' and a learning curve for daughters to practice their art in readiness for adulthood. The thing is they don't know straight away what they can get away with when debating with dad and so they dip their toe in the water at first before jumping in in due course. Top bombing!

For years most dads and daughters have a bond where the little girl will subtly work on making dad proud so that dad will do anything for them. Unaware that the tide is about to turn one day a father is thrust into shock from that first 'nag' and without a seconds hesitation the warning system kicks in and the defense mechanism in his head goes into overdrive, "warning, warning, a new nagger is in the house!"

Men have to laugh when the first feeble attempts at 'nagging' start, normally in the early teens, but occasionally it starts in the kindergarten years for the highly strung ones or those copying mummy who is a dab hand at it. The first efforts are more than likely to do with material things, mobile phones, laptops, iPads, iPods, MacBook's, and eventually clothes!

The early attempts fall into a couple of categories. First is the 'gradual nag' that starts months ahead of birthdays or Christmas. From the old letter to Santa, that kept kids at bay for months, the new verbal list is announced... "I would love one of those for Christmas daddy!" Maybe its not real 'nagging' yet, but July is a bit premature isn't it!

Through the months of August, September, October and November the desired item is brought up again and again with some blinding justifications to why she deserves 'it' and how good she has been. As the festive season approaches the intensity of the 'mini nagging' grows. Despite the conversation on the true expense that takes place, in a pathetic attempt to educate and point out that £200 for a phone and the £36 a month this really means £632 total cost in the first year and another £432 in the second year. Waste of time really as it usually falls on deaf ears. Christmas Day arrives and she unwraps a brand new phone that makes your one look like the original cell phones that resembled a brick in the 1980's...you have given in and you are on a slippery slope!

The second category is the 'silent nag' with the first attempt to make daddy feel guilty by saying nothing. It might start after a father says "no!" when asked if she can go to a sleepover on a school night or to have a tenner and a lift to Pizza Hut to meet her 'friend group'. Whatever the catalyst is, here come the normal angry comments, "just leave it" or "I'm not listening" or "you're not the boss of me" all of which translate to the real meaning of "you better change your mind". Then comes the 'silent nag', a quick stomp and an exit to another room for daddy to contemplate that his little princess is unhappy and whoosh the silent treatment is too much to take, he concedes, albeit with conditions.

The next few years will not only see the physical change from sweet little princess into a man killing machine, it will also see the change from a pleasant little angel into a fully trained professional 'nagger', adept at the one word answers and mind trick comments. Because it's elementary 'nagging' I will only include a few examples, only because they are timid ones.

Well you could afford it if hadn't bought new golf clubs!

Difficult to argue with, but not really the best thing to say to a dad who saved up to replace the hickory shafted hand me downs. A bit of an extreme example maybe but even if it is the new Taylor Made R11 that he clearly needs to get those extra few yards of length off the tee compared to the R9 in his bag, the fact remains that it is HIS money that he earned so it is HIS choice!

Of course the same comment from her mum when he bought the R9 was used as a trade off argument when a couple of hundred pounds appeared on the Amex statement in two thousand and oatcake. All of these strategic comments lead to the same result, daughter gets the desired object...déjà vu or what!

We were talking at school and Ellie's dad is buying her one!

The reverse psychology, a guilt trip and a test of a father's ability to provide what some other poor father has been tricked into. If he says "no" he is a terrible dad, if he says "yes" it probably helps Ellie's quest somewhat and gives her the ammunition to tell her dad that she simply has to have one now, thus a quaint little guilt trip...bloody clever really!

You wouldn't understand, you're too old!

"Ouch!" Yes it might be a few decades since he was her age, but he remembers what it was like growing up as a confused, self-centered little git...nothing has changed there then, maybe he still is?

This type of comment ranks alongside the other old favourites such as "What would you know" and "You know nothing" all said to show the utter disgust at his aged and out of date opinion, which by the way is never welcome either, even if offered in a logical manner with facts presented to educate his offspring.

Whatever immortal phrase is used to cut a proud dad down dead, fathers pick themselves up and try and get to the source of the problem. Big mistake because whatever the problem might be it will obviously be the first time EVER a young girlie has experienced the earth-shattering problem. The end result is pretty uniform though, a barrage of abuse and a slammed door for effect! What the heck, it isn't even something that a dad has done, apart from listening and trying to fix a problem for their little angel. Pow! All of a sudden they are the enemy.

What do they do? Yep, they cross the line and duly enter the inner sanctum of their daughter's bedroom. Opening the door, now with the dodgy hinges, they see a body face down, head buried in a pillow. This is actually an epiphany for the daughter, all of a sudden she realises that she has a 'built in' ability to put a man in his place... to make him follow into the trap "Ooooh!" she says, this is fun, let's practice some more!

The battle plans for the next phase of life are drawn, as if learned in a Military Academy and with a new found confidence in 'self-expression' the art of war begins. Not always those open exchanges either, more the 'covert operations' that win points and ones that occur when brief exchanges between father and daughter are akin to terrorist strikes, shock and awe techniques, 'bang'... mission accomplished.

At a certain adolescent age the teenager diverts attention from dad to new 'raw meat', by that I am referring to rookie boyfriends, who have no idea how to handle the 'nagging' at their tender age, let alone the miserable efforts that older men make all their lives to attempt to deal with a woman's feelings.

After playing with little boys for a few years, hang on disclaimer here as I mean teenage boys over a certain age, they move onto more serious partners that might stick around for a few weeks or months before being dumped for a new target.

Although fathers experience the full brunt of the evolving 'nagger' this is an experience shared by mothers too, often far worse for them. It's quite funny actually when two bunnies with similar DNA are at each other's throats. The Padawan, or the apprentice, versus the Master! Jeez, the combined 'Jedi Mind Tricks' employed by two adversaries for those battles and light sabre exchanges are worth the entry ticket for any bloke. Sorry diverted to Star Wars again and the semi-serious Jedeye Guides that I have written... 'Those aren't the books you are looking for!' (But if you are, check out the suggested further reading at the end of the book... a bit of self promotion!)

So with an introduction to daughters learning their art, we will move onto the next chapter, which is the prelude to marriage, the arranging of the big day.

2
Bride to Be

In the last book I talked about 'Early Doors' when couples first meet, fall hopelessly in love with each other and play Cupids game by spending every minute together or connecting on the phone. It makes your heart glow at the love you see in young couples eyes.

But let us leave the pixie dust in Orlando and resist the temptation to sigh out loud and picture happier days. Back to the journey of life for the young maidens and how daughters gravitate towards earning the equivalent of a bachelors degree in 'nagging' and thus graduate as a learned expert in the art of tying a man up in knots.

Dating, window-shopping and adopting the philosophy of 'try before you buy' all amounts to one day an acceptance that the man of their dreams has been selected. He is now hooked and he is expected to pop the question. After he realises that the barb he is hooked with will simply not come out without a load of pain he decides to leave the barb in, even if it is uncomfortable. Notwithstanding the now required and expected proposal there is a perception that the romantic proposal should be made in the right environment. This place is also part of the dream that a woman may have visualised as a seven year old while dressed as a princess and dreaming of finding a prince. It will be very unlikely

that a castle with a drop dead gorgeous princely character will be a realisation, just the same as the little
boy dreams of proposing to a glamour model, similar
to the one he spotted in a copy of FHM that his dad
hides in the glove compartment of the car!

The perfect location in this dream is unfortunately
an unlikely scene, but a fair compromise is usually
acceptable. It could be on top of a hill next to a white
Greek Ecclesia with views for miles around and with
the warmth of the Cypriot sun adding to the occasion. Alternatively popping the question over dinner
in a plush restaurant, or on a weekend excursion to a
beautiful city might fit the bill too. Another good call
could be at a friends wedding when she is clearly on
a high from the euphoria of seeing her best mate tie
the knot. The giveaway is the apparent determination
in the quest to catch the brides posy, jumping up and,
in what seemed slow motion, clutching the prize bou-
quet snatching it away from the gaggle with masterful
co-ordination, a cracking impression of Trinity in the
"Matrix".

Whatever the dream location or scenario is, the
reality is that the current love of her life has popped
the question, Joy!

Before we move on let's be clear, I'm not saying that
a proposal outside the chip shop is any less romantic
to the perfect couple and I suppose the grease on the
paper can help if the ring presented in a little box is
a tad small for the chubby finger, just ease it on with
the benefit of a bit of lubrication. No, not that! The
ring on her finger, filth!

Shall we assume you get the picture and whatever
the location of the offer, it is accepted and for a short
while 'nagging' is a distant memory?

Or is it? For those religions that seal the contract

with a ring, then a man better be sure that the ring is right, otherwise it can all go horribly wrong.

Any bloke that chooses a ring had better be very sure that the style and value is acceptable. Now a man can do this by watching and listening when she drops a hint here and there. Men should always pay attention to the subtle and abrupt stop outside the jewelers and any reference to the adoration for the three stone white gold beauty. Take note. The other subtle hint is when she passes a comment about the style of a friend's engagement ring. If she doesn't like one stone Cubic Zirconia, best not get one eh? Clever isn't it...but being 100% is not ever going to happen, so roll the dice if you want the surprise element. If not, take the easy option and choose one together at the Jewelery Quarter, but make sure you have enough space on your credit card to satisfy the four figure-shopping spree.

Beware, there is always the potential to drop a testicle or two by guessing, after all she will look at it every day and needs to like and wear it for the next fifty years. Or not as the case may be, but that comes later!

Wedding Planning

After the euphoria and tears of joy shed because she is going to be a bride, a new potential for 'nagging' starts, a new style of 'nagging' which is all to do with the planning of the big day. Obsession can engulf the planning with finer details debated between the newly formed team. This elite planning team is usually recruited within days, if not hours, and is reminiscent of a board of directors headed up by the CEO, the bride. The CEO duly appoints her mother as the Operations Director, and her second reluctant appointment is the

Technical Director, who is his mother and appointed to offer unwelcome counter opinion. Thereafter the second tier appointments are made up of girlfriends and relations.

With the dream team assembled, they take a vote and unanimously agree that each is entitled to 'nag' the groom on any subject, just to keep him in line for the big day. Maybe it isn't a vote at all, perhaps it is a given, after all they are all in charge and their opinion is important and decisions are mandatory, as any strong board of directors are of course.

From nowhere the groom can get chastised for all manner of decisions no matter what creed or religion he is. Before he knows it he will have his attire for the big day chosen. It doesn't matter whether he wanted the charcoal morning wear, a new suit from Next or the Highland Dress with the Buchanan Hunting Tartan; not his choice, it's the Grey Tails with a matching tie that are clearly essential to compliment the Bridesmaids, if not to actually blend in with their dresses.

A schedule is thrust in front of him with mandatory dates that might interfere with his normal schedule. Tough, it's the planning phase and attendance is not only required but integral to the overall project, even if he has no say! Voting rights are not however, therefore he can lodge an opinion but the final hand count will not include his vote. The list is comprehensive with the need to help choose flowers, cars, a venue, cake, and the menu. There is one thing he will certainly not be involved with; The 'Big Secret', yes, what his 'belle' will turn up wearing on the day, the dress.

It might not be this dramatic, but it stands a chance. Of course some couples revel in the joint planning and every decision is made together, well maybe not every, but as the day potentially spirals into something off a reality TV show, it might even need a small mortgage if they are paying out of their own pockets. This is where a comment or two made out of desperation can lead to huge slices of 'nag pie' a good place to start me thinks!

Mum has invited her friends, isn't that great?

"Oh fabulous, the fifty we planned to invite is now going to increase by another ten and my mother will want to ask her friends to balance the room. So that's another twenty."

The wedding breakfast is the biggest sticking point, how many to invite to sit down, consume a meal and share in the drunken speeches? Why it is called a breakfast anyway? If it was just a glorified fry up at a tenner a head then it would be great, but no, this 'breakfast' is a three course meal with coffee and poses further complications for the venue to accommodate the special dietary needs for Aunt Mildred, who is unfortunately coeliac, and cousin Fay, who is a vegan.

Change out of £35 is rare and so every ten extra guests will add considerably to the breakfast bill.

Whether it is a plush venue or a more affordable venue to fit the budget with a menu choice of a few platters of sarnies, cheese on sticks, sausage rolls and slices of quiche the maths is the same; X attendees at Y equals a budget and if X increases the budget is screwed.

Of course all of this assumes that the couple are paying the bill, but even if they are not and either set of parents are contributing, it matters not, it will still be a budget to work too, and even her daddy's cash!

In an attempt to point this out the 'nagging' starts with phrases like "oh really, so I just tell mum they can't come then, that's 'nice' isn't it!" The compromise might be a suggestion that a brilliant cost saving is actually staring them in the face...less invitations to the grooms brood...problem solved!

Do you need to invite all of your family?

"Probably not, but my apologies for my grandmother who clearly enjoyed childbirth and flopped out six aunties and uncles compared to your grandmother who didn't. My bad!"

This links into the first statement of intent, clearly, the guest list is one that should include a mix of friends, as well as a balanced proportion of relatives. Should the groom's headcount reach twice the brides relatives it is a recipe for disaster. Forget the fact that since being together they have been invited to every one of his cousin's weddings, they simply cannot be invited if it puts the family attendees out of kilter. What does he do? Yup, he concedes!

Now risking the 'nagging' from his own mother, he agrees to the final list and counts up the cost of the breakfast again, wishing that it were one with bacon and eggs.

Can you collect the invitations on the way home?

Almost immediately the need to get a piece of card out in the post becomes the postal event of the year. The organising committee will of course choose the perfect gilt edged cards and envelopes, and the task for the groom will probably be to 'pop into the printers, sign the proof off and settle the bill' and then return a week later to pay the balance and collect the printed items. Bearing in mind that the style and design is likely to have been decided without his complete input, when presented with the bill the thought might cross his mind that creating an event on Facebook would be far cheaper, especially with elderly aunts and uncles now his friends on the social media giant. No a bad idea! How uncouth! Task complete and despite the fact that he had nothing to do with the order it is clearly his fault that the printing went wrong and a 'Y' was missed off the second name of his bride to be, "you should have checked when you collected the box, moron!" When this happens the only saving grace is if the signed proof differs from the printed version, a rare escape, especially if the groom signs the proof off!

Invitations reprinted and eventually sent, the venue booked, menu chosen, flowers ordered, cars booked and the all important cake, chosen from the catalogue of examples that included faded photos of two, three and four tier monstrosities, the plans are all in place and for a short time peace reigns.

Peace, that is, until the question of the honeymoon raises its head. If the happy couple are paying for part or all of the big day then the bill is likely to be quite large by now. Adding to the debt with an expensive honeymoon might just tip the savings pot over, but after all it is part of the extravaganza isn't it!

For years the last minute quick getaway with a bargain holiday to a place where the sun has a definite impact on libido is off the agenda. The holiday must be special, and scouring the holiday web sites and brochures narrow the choice down to luxury far off exotic places all inclusive of the ticket price. Why not, he might think, at least it is a one off special type of holiday and so he agrees to say... Barbados in a five star location.

Whether it is a one off honeymoon remains to be seen though, but again that comes later in the book. Even more important is if this is second time around for either the bride or groom, if it is then the second go at a honeymoon better be a big step up from the first one. Bognor to the Almond Beach Club in sunny Barbados, not Barbados to a Best Western, with tea making facilities and en-suite, in Bognor thanks!

Houston...Initiating Countdown

Apart from the ongoing stress that comes with the arrangements and leads to the unavoidable little confrontations on trivial matters, the anticipation of the big day is exciting and bonds the happy couple together, hopefully!

With a few weeks to go the focus turns to the hen and stag nights, which is the bachelorette party and bachelor party for our American cousins reading this. These two events can cause more anguish than anything else. Forget the fact that the couple have committed to a life together, with thousands of notes spent on one day. Oh no, for some reason the seed of doubt creeps in and the opportunity to 'do someone' before the vows are taken is clearly what is going to happen.

Why is this? Probably because we have all seen whatever the collective noun is for a group of women on a hen night, 'cluckers' perhaps, and the antics that revolve around binge drinking and snogging any bloke that passes by. The same is said for the stags, who work as a pack of wolves encircling women and pleading that their man is in need of a snog, a quickie in the fire exit or to emulate Shalamar's lyrics and make it one last "night to remember" for him, all because he will soon be legally joined at the hip to his bride.

Whether all hens and all stags actually do go out with the intention of fulfilling a last night of freedom is irrelevant. The trust factor is put to the test and from this worry comes some lovely 'nagging' comments, very similar to the chapter on cross examination in the first book. Similar, but let's not try and kid ourselves, the comments are far more intense for this one night in a couples relationship.

Although men have the same concerns over their fiancée being encouraged to joyfully receive a slap from some strangers dangly bits in their face, or get blind drunk and do something that they may regret, they are far more relaxed before the hen night than women. Both the bride and bridegroom will put a marker or two down and so I suppose these next few comments are more unisex, albeit conjured up by a woman first!

Have a good time

Means, have a boring time, don't talk to anyone of the opposite sex and only have a few drinks! Another Jedi Mind Trick, "this isn't the fun night you're looking for." Said in Sir Alec Guinness stylee with the classic mid chest height swipe of a hand to cast the spell!

What time are you coming home?

Oh boy, the time limit comment and a commitment to be home by a predefined time. Said so that it will stick in his mind every time he looks at his watch, until that is he can only see four circles where there was once one and time is irrelevant now.

Committing to being home by a certain time is a recipe for disaster, unless he intends to get back way before the stated time, crawl up the driveway, leaving enough time to negotiate the key and lock problem that miraculously occurs when bladdered. Why doesn't the damn key ever fit? Yuri Geller has been messing with it obviously!

Going past the stated time leaves him open for the cross examination, damming evidence so he must be aware not to say or commit to anything that leaves him open to the risk of wrath. A perfect answer is "all depends on the availability of taxis at chuck out time really, my sweet".

Behave yourself

"Of course I will darling, as opposed to being let off the leash and flagrantly back scuttling anything that has a pulse!"

What is that all about? Is it a veiled threat with the obvious temptation that will make him misbehave because he is out with friends instead of under her beady eye?

Trust or trussed? Time to choose but remember that most stags are committed to their fiancé and un-less she trusts him now she may as well bind him up in gaffer tape securely because he obviously doesn't have the willpower to stop himself doing the dirty on her! Time to choose honey.

Shall we all meet up later?

The test question, to see if his friends are on a mission to get him into an embarrassing situation they can all then snigger about at the wedding. This suggestion is tantamount to giving him a pass for a few hours but the doubt over what happens when he is out for a few extra minutes longer is too much to take. The obvious suggestion is to therefore have the stags meet up with the hens before it gets too crazy. Genius! What a way to start married life, but for some couples meeting up could be the perfect option.

If this suggestion is made and he prefers not to go along with it then it probably means that he has something to hide, or even if he is actually innocent or that his organising committee has tipped him the wink that there is a plan afoot. Stuck between plausible deniability before the stag do and real concern that his crew have project managed the night, with an evil plot to entertain the collective stags!

Sometimes the suggestion to meet up is made during the night, a text message sent just as he has hit the point of no return and the alcohol gives him superpowers and a new level of independence, "sod that" he slurs "I'm having a great time!"

Whether he ends up in the gutter, gagged and tied to a lamppost or strapped to a bed, face down, with someone dressed up as Superman standing over him is really irrelevant. Sorry, I digressed to a picture in my mind and a story about someone's stag night, very disturbing, censored and most definitely wrong! Yes SuperMAN not SuperGIRL before you question it. Back on track, thankfully, the aftermath is going to be difficult, in some cases this can bring on a newly defined stress condition called 'post traumatic nag disorder' PTND that is! Not too much research has been done on this newly stated condition, if any, but it could be the future field of research for this author to get into!

I will know, you know

Back to the mind reading skills that we covered in the first book and how women have and the ability to know a man's darkest secrets, or at least pretend to know what skeletons he hides in that closet of his.

Let's face it this is another shot across the bows just before he goes out; one to let him know that she might know if he does something, so best not to cross any line and risk being caught doing something that you didn't do, but might have done without knowing it.

Although these are all comments to test him before

he goes out, the real potential for 'nagging' comes the next morning. Again I will leave the cross-examination questions out here, as I mentioned them in the first book, and concentrate on some little gems that come out specifically after the hen night or stag night. See, I am still maintaining that unisex approach, or at least hiding behind the fact that women usually direct it at men, or should I say at the bridegroom by the bride.

So what happened?

Here we go, straight in with the killer question. Even if the night was relatively tame, the prerequisite for a full and frank disclosure is needed. Perfect timing on her part after a late night full and copious amounts of alcohol.

A good way to disguise the fact that a stag cannot remember much is to clasp his hand over his mouth and rush to the toilet. However this ploy is temporary and at some point he will need to gather his thoughts and rack a brain cell or two to come out with the answers.

Bearing in mind that the 'bride to be' perhaps knows the sordid details because the girlfriend of one of his so-called mates might have texted her with an exaggerated account of the shenanigans. A level of caution is required until he can work out first whether anything happened he should be ashamed of and then second which one of his fellow stags is weak enough to say anything derogatory. If a candidate from the group is identified quickly it might be narrowed down to the lily-livered poof with a soft patch where his balls used to be. Crap! the stag may then wonder whether gob almighty might be so weak that he would pee his pants if questioned by his partner thus the possibility casts more doubt and further caution is required.

This caution turns to panic if the bleary mind fabricates a suggestion of what garbage might have been blarted out by the coward to save his own bacon. But the stag doesn't know and more importantly he really can't remember if the taxi driver was actually one of his old flames that happened to be in the bar, by chance of course. Ouch head throbbing he is stuck in short-term memory loss mode.

What does he do? Tell her what he remembers and take a slice of 'nag pie' to get it over with or protest his innocence because that is the truth? The truth will out even if the majority of the night was innocent, there will be a few funnies that occurred. "So what" he may feel, after all it was a night out to celebrate the fact that he is soon to be married. That is fine as long as the truth is innocent with a little bit of humiliation at the hands of the group, but if it is less than innocent and involved tonsil tennis, a fumble or full blown whatever then he should expect a grilling.

Depending on how and what he says, and indeed remembers, then the secondary questioning is likely to major on the one small thing he was goaded into by the group and that lasted a few seconds compared to the six hours thirty nine minutes from leaving the house to sleeping in the porch, he was out having innocent fun. No matter the misdemeanor is out, whatever it is.

To be honest the vast majority of stags and hens are incapable of doing anything really bad by about ten o'clock. However long the night went on for they could probably plead insanity because of their inability to stand, think, talk, walk, touch or sense anything.

For many years I witnessed the stag and hen parties from the relatively safe position behind a set of decks in nightclubs. This was a great place to see just how drunk and incapable people can get and how innocent most parties are. Hen parties were like a night out for a Roman Maniple, maybe not 120 strong, but any sign of insurgence from a group of men would lead to shields up and into 'formation' to protect the hen. The stags, on the other hand usually resembled a tribe of unorganised heathens, moving en masse towards groups of women, shouting collectively while eventually breaking ranks and dispersing to be picked off by the doormen or even worse groups of less desirable women.

Yes, for sure some stag parties had little games afoot, such as 'pull a pig' or 'embarrass the groom' or even 'dares for drinks'. Lame games apart from the aftermath of 'pull a pig' that unfortunately upset ugly people who thought they have a chance with a good looking bloke, but were unaware of the game being played. Very naughty!

Analysis and opinion out of the way, back to the real stuff. The 'nagging' which can be a bit one-sided when it comes to the events at the stag night compared to the innocence of the hens on tour. What is a wee bit unfair is when the stag is assumed to have done something and is justified in taking a 'word beating' to make sure, whereas when the groom asks the same question all hell breaks loose. How dare he question what happened, where they went or whom they saw?

Why do women react this way, is there anything to hide or is it part of the game to keep a man guessing? Hmmm, it could be a way of playing on insecurities, inciting the green monster and to give them some doubt, keep them on their toes and not take a woman for granted.

The Big Day

Thankfully, in most cases, what happened on tour stayed on tour or as nothing happened anyway the focus moves to the Big Day itself.

The organising committee will have planned everything down to the size of the petals and number of posies required and all that remains to be done for the groom is to turn up and say "yes." Simple enough but we all know that the potential for things to go wrong is ever present and blame is likely to be aimed in the form of an outburst or two.

The groom will have an itinerary to follow which will start with getting up and ready in plenty of time, god forbid he is late and sleeps in. There might be a need to collect something from the florist, baker or Aunt Gladys who is coming down from Grangemouth on the 6am train to save a night in a hotel. Whatever the list of tasks are it is imperative that he completes them in full and on time.

The night before he will no doubt receive a prompt and as he is handed the list by his beau; she will go through the list one by one just to make sure that he understands what he needs to do. Why? Is it because in thinking about taking his vows he has lost the ability to read the list? Yes that will be it.

If the traditional approach is adopted the couple will have to spend the night apart and the groom may have to sleep at his mothers for a night, great preparation for married life isn't it. A night with mother throwing a comment or two in about being sure that he wants to go through with it perhaps or that 'she' is not good enough for 'him'. How rude! Mother might have a little dig about the imbalance of guests in favour of the brides family and friends.

Even though the discussion on the need to control numbers has been had more times than she has used incontinence pants. The fact remains that his mother wanted Dot to be there and the happy couple didn't have the courtesy to invite her.

Don't be Late!

Just in case he is relaxed despite the copious amounts of stewed tea that his mother has brewed in an attempt to mother her son for the last time, he might get a call just before bedtime and the last minute nerves might generate a comment or two, however they don't count as real nagging as the euphoria of the predicted perfect day overcomes the need to take any umbrage in a comment directed at the groom. The one comment that is almost a cliché is "don't be late" and in truth it works both ways but when directed at the groom it is a warning to, most definitely, get there on time and in a sober state. This is not the case for the bride by the way who is perfectly entitled to be fashionably late.

The parting conversation usually ends with a "see you tomorrow MRS X" and reciprocated by the giggling bride to be with a "see you tomorrow MR X" aw isn't it cute and lovely.

Confetti Heaven

Despite the temptation to throw in some spurious satirical examples of nagging that might take place around the ceremony itself, let us instead go with the majority of wonderful weddings whereby the ceremony goes perfectly. A slip of the tongue by a nervous bride or groom is totally is acceptable, unless the words get fuzzled and come out in the wrong order that is. The wrong name is however not so good. It happens, but is worse when the wrong name used is an old flame!

Sorry off I go again on the fiction trail, or is it? Hmmm, distinctly remember a few occasions when the wrong name has been used when addressing me and, in truth, occasionally I may have used an innocent word in a sentence that SOUNDS LIKE a name of an ex! For example the morning I asked the 'love of my life' if she fancied a cuppa and said, "tea now?', which in her half awake state she deciphered as 'Tina,' wife number one by the way, yes a cup of char that turned into a suggestion that I had called her the wrong name, how that went down like a burning Spitfire... But that's not important now as indeed it wasn't at the time, like hell it wasn't!

Back to the wedding day, let us imagine that the now legal contract is binding and made openly in front of witnesses with the vows said without any slip up's.

On the subject of traditional vows and the wording, much has been said over the Christian 'honour and obey' promises in the last few decades and how the words are nonsense in this day and age with more and more couples electing to remove the promise from the vows. In truth this is probably right as the swing towards equality has somewhat nullified this promise that a woman would break pretty quickly nowadays.

There isn't anything in the vows about agreeing 'nagging' as part of the relationship contract is there? Perhaps this needs addressing by the church and all other religions to include something in the man's vows such as "to accept criticism and questioning without recourse" or "honour my end of the bargain but also accept that I have done something wrong when clearly I haven't" makes sense to me in whatever language it is translated into.

For the girlies, something like, "to trust with the

option to cross-examine, probe for the truth or to make something up that justifies my sixth sense." Yes that would work perfectly.

Until the wording is clarified in this litigious world that we live in, we will have to accept that it is an unwritten undertaking and precedent is set so men cannot use the argument that they were not aware that 'nagging' is an acceptable part of a marriage.

Breakfast is Served

Moving on. So the ecstatic couple have done the deed, no wait the consummation comes later probably. They have stated their love and commitment for the rest of their lives and the day moves on from the ceremony to the reception. This is where the family get together can certainly cause some problems and the potential for 'nagging' returns after the lull of the last few months for the groom. The good thing for the groom is that the bride will have multiple targets to concentrate on during the build up, say hotel staff, the wedding dress alteration specialist or the video production company boss.

So what is the catalyst for 'wedding day nagging'? Well it's a combination of guests that can't control their drinking, missing guests from the photo call and cutting comments from one side of the family, let alone the potential punch up that is reminiscent of a televised encounter on the set of Jeremy Kyle!

Families, oh my, they can be a nightmare. The cantankerous Great Auntie that upsets everyone she talks to because of her jealousy of her sister that did far better in life. Perhaps the jilted cousin who hates to see anyone happy after being dropped like a hot potato five years ago by the bloke who saw sense and recognised the potential for devastating 'nagging' and legged it to avoid a life of strife. She has now found solace in food, chocolate and doughnuts to be exact and is a bit of a recluse now.

As is customary at these things, before the bride and groom have a chance to sit down and partake in a tipple the obligatory photo call is required and it stands a chance that the bride will take over as the director at some stage. The poor photographer will have clear instructions issued to snap a photo of her and her girlies, one to placate the cantankerous aunties and another with her third and fourth cousins that she hasn't seen in a decade or two. Now this is where the direction can turn into the first 'nag' of married life. The happy hubby is dispatched to find the missing relative by the missus. Returning a few minutes later he hears the first negative remark since, well he can't remember really, "where have you been? At the bar no doubt, I ask you to do one small thing and you wander off!" Welcome to a new world.

Speeches ...Tin Hat Required!

Meal served and consumed, the alcohol flowing freely, Great Aunt Mildred probably half cut after a third sherry, it is nearly time for the speeches and as far as the groom is concerned there are three potential minefields to negotiate. First the new father in law, then his own and finally his best man. Maybe it's time for a tin hat, as a precaution.

Developing a false laugh is a skill that many a groom should practice before the wedding day. To laugh at the appropriate time when the father in law gets to his feet and starts on an emotional account of how he has had to give up his darling daughter to, in his opinion, a less than desirable husband. If dad goes off on an embarrassing diatribe about his hope that his daughter would always marry a cardiologist not a struggling salesman and the groom doesn't laugh in the right place then he might be up for a telling off for being too sensitive. This is one of the rare times in his life when he is likely to get a public dig from a bloke which he is not allowed to react to.

In most cases thankfully the father in law is perfectly happy to pass over the responsibility and spending habits of his mouthy daughter to another man, finally!

After the applause and perhaps even a tear or two from his doting daughter it is the grooms turn. With bated breath he must now deliver a perfect speech. Thanking the right people in the right order and also stating how beautiful his bride looks is a must. If done without a pre-written speech this is asking for trouble, but any mistakes, errors, missing name checks are likely to be rectified if the bride takes the more modern approach and takes her turn to speak... Oh god, three glasses of bubbly, wine, desert wine and a Drambuie is a recipe for disaster.

For the first time, as Mrs X, she relishes the challenge and to speak for her husband in public. With a critical tone she will apologise for his cock up in missing someone out, so in essence this is a bit of 'public nagging', but best let everyone know who wears the trousers now. If Mrs X adopts the traditional standpoint then any mistakes will be saved up for a quiet moment later!

Two down and with not too much collateral damage it can lull the groom into a false sense of security, why? Because his best man is about to deliver a well rehearsed stand up routine and he knows that he is going to be the brunt of the jokes, nowhere to hide and no idea of the content of the well guarded pages of notes.

Needless to say that if the content includes any surprises for Mrs X, any important details that the best man exposes from previous life such as the stag do, then the backlash might just spoil the day. Even if the speech is delivered with decorum and is intentionally non descript there might be something in there that will raise a question or two, especially if it was when our now blushing groom was on an 18-30 holiday and three in a bed, which by the way was normal behavior back then!

As the best man raises his glass to the bridesmaids, even the one who looks like she has eaten one of the others, and everyone stands to join in with the toast, if the groom receives a glaring look, a boney elbow in the side or a stiletto heel to the polished shoes it is a sign that the subject will be raised ... maybe not straight away, but soon. The hint that a bit of 'nagging' is coming his way is when he returns to the seated position and the immortal words are whispered, "we will talk about this later!" oh great she is pissed off, even if the secret uncovered was ten years before they got together. Fanbleedingtastic!

How many weddings go this way? Not many but when they do and as a guest watching from the sidelines it is hilarious. It can also prompt a tote amongst the rest of the guests on how long before they split up for some 'space' ...game on, certainly worth a £5 pledge to the tote with a quick reserve on the six month maximum box, before one of the aunties swoop down and choose the same length of time to reinforce what they said at the church before hand too.

The mix of euphoria and drink should lead to a great night and the only problem could be too much partying and passing out before consummating the marriage, brewers droop is either a welcome excuse for a woman to pass out herself or something that will haunt a man for decades if she takes offence. Indeed the perfect time to move onto the next Chapter, which assumes years of married bliss, setting up home and more family gatherings.

3
Homemaking

These days the vast majority of couples have moved in together or plan to move in together straight after the wedding, not all but most have gone through the trauma of buying a house or finding a suitable place to rent.

Homemaking includes buying stuff together and unwrapping the wedding presents in the hope that the list has been fulfilled and the set of Jamie Oliver Little Tinker dinner plates is complete, along with the roaster and salad plates. Nothing worse than having three of one and five of the other, that means having to spend vouchers to complete the set. A far cry from the Eternal Bow collection and electric carving knife requested twenty something years ago.

There could be a few missing items and the obligatory pressie from Great Aunt Mildred that wasn't on the list, but there is a use for a bedspread in the future guest bedroom; actually no, unless the décor planned is retro 1930's that is. Amazing what you can get at the church bazaar nowadays.

With more boxes than you would find in a Thai whorehouse littering the spare room, the task in hand is to find a place to put the recently acquired items in the all too little abode. Built in wardrobes are the favourite until the father in law decides to clear the loft and bedroom, once occupied by his daughter, depositing a dozen large removal sized boxes in the spare bedroom while the couple were in Barbados. Is this something that fathers do as a cleansing exercise at losing their daughter to another man? Or is it the mother in law that takes the opportunity to 'nag' him a little to clear out the wardrobe that she wants back after all of these years to now store her marmalade?

Whatever the reason for this bizarre ritual, the arrival of boxes that are all full of memories can prompt some negative comments between the love struck couple. Never mind that the boxes contain odd inanimate objects that include a selection of designer clothes, acrylic jumpers, and accessories purchased on a whim to complete the outfits and replicate the Burton's or Top Shop manikin from the shop window when she was 18. It stands a chance that any clear out will contain other contentious items that were stuffed into a shoe box a decade or more ago; such as the collection of cassettes, mix tapes put together by previous boyfriends and in a really sweet but rather pathetic attempt to include a collection of love tunes that meant so much way back then. Memorex C90's with a handwritten running order and little hearts drawn on in are now almost illegible with only a hint of faded red biro. Costume jewelery is another old favourite here and an old plastic box from Ratners or H Samuel could hold a collection of dangly earrings, once gold but now light green.

In the days before Facebook and email people had two options to communicate, telephone and letters. For some reading this it probably sounds incredible that these were the only two options and included the use of a pen for the latter, but it is true and even more incredible it actually worked. With this in mind, letters were often stored away so that the time delay in an envelope being posted and then delivered meant that anything in a reply might refer to the letter previously sent, so all letters needed to be kept for reference purposes. In short a filing system that didn't really get used that much. It therefore stands a real chance that letters written from a first holiday romance, when she was 14, could include one from Fernando the waiter and then some from Carlos, the bell boy, a year later.

Although couples do generally sift through the discarded memories when parents thrust the hoarded collection on the newly married couple, the problem starts when some little private gems rear their ugly head. From a cute little conversation over the way Fernando declared his love, in broken English for a month or two before zoning in on a new holiday maker, other pictorial memories can raise a question or two that are potentially interpreted as an invasion of previous privacy!

Forget the faded student bus pass that now looks nothing like how she looks today, it is the pack of Boots photos with a disintegrated rubber band that has stuck to the glossy envelope and more importantly contains pictures of her first girly holiday. Whether the pack contains one or two piccies of the first time she had the courage to go topless or the less flattering ones of her legless after consuming half a bottle of 7 Star Metaxa, it was forever ago. Not even the funny photo with her as a youthful girl being dry humped by her first true holiday romancer, Steve from Sheffield. It is all well and good if she openly shares the images, but if she hurriedly hides the pack away, it is cause for concern. Does it matter? Of course not but for some reason it is private and probably brings back feelings that certainly don't require justification.

On the other hand if a man has a small box of memories that his mother has put together after clearing her own antique wardrobe, it is a different scenario. Just suppose that the Fyffes banana box also contains a collection of Boots photo packets, one labelled Club 18-30 with Dave. Now this is the same holiday as mentioned in the speeches all those weeks ago and she wants to take a look to identify whomever and get some evidence. Oh crap, that old chestnut!

"Let's have a look then" she might say with a false smile and nonchalant expression, she needs to know the details, even if he isn't privy to her sordid secrets. More disturbing evidence might be hidden in his discarded trinkets and god forbid his mother hasn't mistakenly dropped in a wedding photo from his first albeit brief marriage; she wouldn't do that would she? Probably! It stands a chance that if there is anything that could cause offence it will and likely generate the following comments, as she thumbs through the images, pausing at those with another female in the shot and speeding up when the ones of the hotel from the room or the peninsular captured from the glass bottomed boat are of no interest to her, before taking a second pass at the offending ones again.

So which ones did you sleep with?

"Neither my darling I didn't score that holiday"
A bad move because his best man has already indicated that is a lie and his attempts to explain that it was playful banter and fiction have already failed.

Furthermore the description of the offending twins fits the drunken interrogation of the best man on the wedding day. Information will be stored, just for the moment though as it will likely be brought up in good time.

Well we haven't got room for your stuff so shall I get a bin bag?

What the frick, hang on a few shoe boxes of memories that he may or may not look at again until he is older versus twelve crates of hers and she wants the sordid evidence black bagged. Yes that works doesn't it?

Suggesting that the exercise is futile and perhaps she could start chucking the plastic belts out to make some space will likely fall on deaf ears. If a man does decide to take it on himself to bag and store items then he had better remember which box went into which black bag.

Are you saying you want to keep all this? Why?

The test question, if he wants to keep it why? He is married now and silly things have no place in a trusting marriage. As if it is any threat, jeez. A sign of things to come?

You didn't tell me about this

"Hang on, the subject of numbers and ranking past conquests is a 'no go area' that was established very quickly in the relationship. Leave it at that."

Not happening. The evidence is clear and so what if it happened at roughly the same time as Steve from Sheffield was nestling his mullet hairdo in her ample cleavage in Magaluf, it is an IMPORTANT piece of information that should have been shared. Why there is an imbalance in this 'ancient history reveal'? It is something that never fails to shock men. Thou must declare all and not ask of me my wrongdoings... if they can be actually treated as wrongdoings that is, who gives a damn anyway? Err, she does!

Homemaking thus includes planning for the future and accepting previous life occurrences that might include items brought into the marital home that either find a place on the mantelpiece or are stored in a wardrobe never to be seen again!

The first book includes some classic DIY comments and here we go with a few more that revolve around homemaking, and again some alternative answers that a man would dearly love to say.

My dad would have done it better
"I'm sure he would, after all he is perfect in your eyes my sweet!"

Yes, fathers do DIY better than fledgling husbands, especially if they are a decorator by trade. But at least 'having a go' should demonstrate the intention to paint, paper or preserve the home. Attempting is surely worth some brownie points and you never know with practice a fledgling might actually get better and match the high standards of the fully-grown eagle father in law. Hang on, eagle father? Daughter is a bird of prey!

Shall I just get dad to do it?
"Why not, I am sure he would love to do it right anyway and I suppose that it will stop him having to lie when he inspects it with a critical eye next Sunday as he nibbles on a brussel sprout."

Another slur on a man's ability to do it right and a cutting comment to ensure that a new husband is aware of the pecking order of life, father first and him second.

On the positive side of life getting the father in law in to do stuff, properly, is not a bad idea and might free up some time to pop out with the lads for 18 holes. Wait a second, no, help from the father in law probably means working for him as his bitch for the day, holding stuff while he works, passing the right professional tools and making sure he doesn't topple over by being the human anchor for the step ladder for hours on end. Might as well learn from the master though, just the same as you did as a ten year old for your own father, and act as an apprentice for the day in the hope that the surrogate father is sympathetic to the inadequacies that you demonstrated in the first place.

You said you could fix it

"Yes I did, but didn't realise that the previous occupant was a cowboy, perhaps the giveaway was the use of a six shooter staple gun to keep the coving wedged against the ceiling."

For any man, repairing a botched initial job by the previous owner this somehow means that the original sin against the property is actually his own doing. Behind every roll of wallpaper there is potential for a multitude of problems with the plaster. Only when the wallpaper stripper melts the paste as well as the glue used to hold the wall together does the problem actually show up.

From an early age boys play with toys that teach and nurture their ambition to grow up into a fixer. Men like to show women that they can mend things and put things right. Unfortunately some men are not blessed with the skills to carry out the task without having to adopt some mini fix it's, such as the wedge of folded paper covered with copious amounts of quick dry filler. Filler and rapid dry glue is a man's best friend in DIY projects closely followed by beading, an invention that covers up gaps as well as slight discrepancies. It is true to say that beading is probably one of the finest inventions and one that even fathers use to extreme.

When things go wrong with any DIY project it can result in a lot of huffing and puffing. How often does a ten-minute DIY job turn into a couple of hours? Quite a lot, but here's the thing the challenge for a man is to work out how to make it right and in a way that doesn't leave a visual sign of a botched job for their better half. Disguising the problem requires a well rehearsed set of lines to first offer a technical explanation of the problem and second a suggestion that he can make it right so best leave him to it eh? All rehearsed to baffle a woman and gain a bit more time while he tries to work out how to do it.

Hiding Things

Homemaking isn't just about decorating or fitting clothes into the small wardrobe spaces available. It is also about taking pride in the appearance and cleanliness of the shack. Keeping the place clean means regular vacuuming, dusting and other girlie jobs that men should want to do too. Indeed the weekends might include a bit of time bonding while a couple work as a team tidying up a room at a time.

Tidying up is all too often it is the expectation from one or the other to run the vacuum over the lounge carpet without the need for instruction to do so. It is made worse when one has OCD, Obsessive Compulsive Disorder, and is rarely without a duster or trigger spray in their hands.

The problem of acceptable levels of cleanliness is where some severe 'nagging' takes place, and a few examples follow this bit of analysis.

But as well as the expectation to do more tidying up there is the risk that a man who isn't under direction from a woman will move things and clearly hide things from her.

Where have you put it?

Even if a man is innocent of moving anything and a woman has tidied it up herself, a man is prime suspect for the missing item.

Whether it is a piece of paper, her keys, her parents keys, a lipstick or an envelope, it doesn't matter what it is that a man has tidied up, he had better remember where he has put it and hurry off to find it now!

The envelope is the biggest item at risk of being lost forever, especially when someone has the habit of opening her post and for a completely crazy reason put the contents back into the opened envelope after she has read it. Why do people do that? Is it a way to maintain security or is it to protect the contents in some way? The house will probably have a place where opened post lives and it stands a chance that the leaflet from the pizza company will sit amidst the opened envelopes too, therefore when the recycling box needs filling the pizza deal and what appears to be an old envelope can end up in the green box.

The safest place for anything that a man tidies up is the 'everything drawer' located in the kitchen and although originally designed to house the matching utensils when the kitchen was fitted, it now plays host to envelopes, hair bobbles, petrol receipts, Red Cross pens, paper-clips, Sellotape, rubber bands, blue mascara, black mascara, pink lip gloss, 'hooker' red lip gloss, dead batteries, working batteries, paper clips, drawing pins, a Pritt Stick, a pack of second class stamps, a travel adapter, chewing gum and even Blu Tack! It is a safe haven but over time the paper may not fit in and a clear out is usually needed before the envelopes spill over the back of the drawer and end up in the void behind the unit...in fact this could be where the missing item is...genius!

What have I told you, don't ever throw my things out!

"Oh wonderful now I am guilty and until proving my innocence that anything that is missing has been obviously cleared out and binned; the evidence is conclusive, end of case. Hang me then!"

The problem occurs because of the one occasion when a man has emptied the waste paper bins or taken it upon himself to discard the unwanted contents of the everything drawer because he couldn't close it anymore. Unaware that the flyer with a voucher for the nail bar WAS needed and HE erroneously threw it out and therefore by definition and as the obvious precedent, he might have chucked anything that is now missing.

The answer is simple, aha! Have an 'everything box' and put things that he might be tempted to throw away into the box instead. Very clever, until the garage gets taken over by boxes of saved items that now live with the boxes deposited by her father from her old room that have migrated to the garage by now.

This genius solution however can mean that there is now a real excuse not to throw anything out and thus contribute to the hacking down of rainforest's trees instead of fueling the recycling that we are all encouraged to do. Piles of cashpoint advices, parking tickets, debit card receipts and even Boots vouchers can soon take up box space and in turn actually put the required piece of paper in jeopardy of being lost in a pile, which of course will be the man's fault as well.

Encouraging a woman to clear out the 'everything drawer' and collection of 'everything boxes' is tantamount to asking her to throw out the Crown Jewels! For some reason these mini records are important and should be kept, just in case. The net result is that five years down the line when she does go through stuff she will probably utter the words, "I wondered where that was, oh damn the offer has expired" and indeed it probably has if it was dated four years ago.

This fundamental difference between a man and a woman is abundantly clear when we don't think twice about throwing something out, a statement, a guarantee or a 'two for one offer', only to chunter at a later date when we need the discarded item and then have to try and get a copy. Wasted time but at least we really need it at some stage.

What happened to that bin bag in the utility room?

Oh crap, the bin bag that contained a selection of clothes destined for the ironing lady, the one that had her winter boots in or even the 'to keep' papers that should have been put in the garage. How many times has a man inadvertently seen the bag and ASSUMED that it was there for the weekly bin run, failing to look inside because the gaffer tape around the top was bound so tightly that it must be rubbish? In an attempt to carry out the weekly chore delegated as HIS job, putting the bins out, he may have thrown out the black bag in question and he is in the crap now!

Sods Law confirms the fact that the question is asked not in the five days that the bag sat in the corner but on the day after the big green wagon emptied the wheelie bin.

There is no escaping the grief he will receive, and quite right too I hear you say, how stupid is it to throw out a bag without checking first. Maybe next time eh!

Finding Things

Forget the mild 'nagging' that comes with hiding things, let us look at the cringe worthy and painful experience that a man or woman enjoys when their partner finds something. It stands a very good chance that everyone reading this will recognise this, maybe from experience and especially when a woman finds something. In fairness the 'thing' found might be an inanimate object, but it can symbolise cheating, lies and the use of the last chance card. Assuming that it is really bad then how can anyone defend it? Well they can't but sometimes that creative brain inside a woman's head quickly finds a mole and convinces the mole to make a mountain in double quick time!

Women assume that men want to get found out and thus hide things in places that they know women regularly check. This makes sense now, and in hiding things in crap places they secretly want to get a little bit of extra 'nagging'. Sorted!

Trousers left draped over a chair, jeans in the washing basket, a coat on the balustrade or the top pocket of a shirt are all hiding places for items of deception, pieces of paper that require explanations when they point to secrets.

What's this? A betting slip

"Yes, suppose the Ladbrokes logo is a giveaway...and?"
Putting a tenner on a different type of nag is what a vast proportion of the male species actually do, a bit of fun and a risk with potential reward. If however it isn't an agreed spend from the family coffers it is very naughty and deserves a reprimand. Isn't it amazing though how the winning betting slips are accepted, especially if the proceeds are used to take a woman out for a slap up meal?

Why did you take out £200 from the cashpoint?

"Let me get this straight, £200 of my money from my account? Probably because I can, and needed to after you rifled my wallet of every note to pay the Betterware lady!"
If a man withdraws a couple of hundred pounds then he must be siphoning cash for something, forget the twenty given to his daughter, ten for emergency milk and a microwave Chinese meal for two, thirty for a couple of bottles of plonk, another twenty for two lots of window cleaning and at least fifty to replace the pilfered emergency cash that he always carries around. It really is amazing where cash goes, but to have to account for every fiver is nuts! If a man turns this around and asks a woman to account for her own cash withdrawals then he can expect the invasion of privacy comment, how dare a man question where a woman spends money. That is outrageous!

Receipts from Tiffany, buying your secretary something nice were you?

"You weren't meant to see that, my bad, but let me see we are in December and there is an important date coming up where a little blue box might be appreciated by a certain spouse…if you don't want it I can use it to get into my PA's knickers though, only if you don't mind that is!"
It is an elementary error that men make, it's much better to hide receipts before Christmas, birthdays, anniversaries and any other day that involves a wrapped item.

On the other hand, if the receipt is a credit or debit card receipt for £34 from a bar then expect that a woman might think that the five pints of lager, a Magners with ice and three bottles of Corona with lime, was actually a bottle of Veuve Cliquot bought to impress a bunch of girls in the bar, not the round that he had to buy on a card was because he had no cash after the fairies rifled his wallet earlier.

In an open relationship surely there is absolutely no need to justify a grown up decision to buy something that is needed but for some reason it is required by some couples and so a detailed till receipt can certainly help the defense if questioned. Yes it might add to the everything drawer with additional bits of paper but best to just staple it to the credit card, there's a good boy!

I found a lighter in your jeans

"Bah, rumbled and I bet you think I'm smoking again, but you would be wrong, the BBQ needs igniting and I was out of flint and tinder fungus and to boot the steel rod needed to create the spark was sticking out of my back from my last faux par!"

Another difficult one to explain, and whether it is a receipt for a newspaper, a Snickers and 10 Marly Lights that the previous patron inadvertently left on top of the pile of Sunday Express's and he then gathered up with his copy by mistake or alternatively a box of Swan Vesta's found in his coat, it is a sign that must mean he is having a crafty fag on the quite.

What the hell are you doing with the Little Book of Hugs in your briefcase?

"Umm … It was lent to me?"

Pathetic reply and if the object found has any reference to what another woman could have given a man as a heart felt pressie then what can a man say? Very little, even if the truth is that it is harmless. Yes I know the specific example is a bit strange for say another person to lend one of those hardback Forever Friends books that kids buy mum for Mothers Day. Strange as it might be that the ulterior motive could be to share the offending item with another parent or to remind that person to buy one for his wife. It isn't however very good if the book falls out of his briefcase before the surprise, or she finds it when looking for the joint account chequebook!

What is it about the little yet over priced toys, pens, key rings or mugs that are the mainstay of Clintons Cards turnover? After all they normally end up in the 'everything drawer' anyway so if people exchange for the most innocent of reasons, why are they so important? Jeez its not like they are blue Tiffany boxes or worse, something for the weekend. There I am glad, I finally got that off my chest! Bit late, but innocence protested, what a numpty for borrowing it in the first place.

Cleaning up...After Yourself

As I mentioned before keeping the home neat and tidy is where most couples agree, some however disagree and unless they are both content to live in a turd fest then it stands a chance that there is an expectation to run the vacuum over the floor regularly and not to a diary schedule, if it needs it, do it!

This fundamental task aside, there is the potential for a falling out if one or other adopts the policy to hang things up and the other to utilise the door handles, chair or the floor instead. Now there might be a valid reason for the need to use the available external hanging space, especially if the wardrobe space allocated to the man is far less than to the woman. Over the years what was once his side often becomes their shared wardrobe, why? Because her side is full and despite the need to bag never worn clothes, they still reside on the Johnsons hanger with the dry cleaning slip pinned to the lapel. The space issue compounded by the fact that the items are not only still in the plastic bag, but also that they need to be hung in the tall bit and thus the split shelf was taken out to allow dresses and trousers to hang properly, thus leaving adequate space at the bottom for the excess plastic bagging as well.

This doesn't alter the fact that over time a woman's clothes collection encroaches on a man's own wardrobe space. The logical thing to do is clearly to avoid the frustration of trying to wedge a hanger, with a pair of trousers on, into a gap on the rail but instead drape the trousers over a chair. Perfect!

Drawing the line at boxer shorts and socks on the floor is completely expected though. The laundry basket is where smellies go and this should be used at every turn. On the subject of undies a man that clears up any bra hooked to the back of the door faces the wrath of a woman; if he puts it in the laundry basket, it will come into contact with his boxer shorts, disgusting especially when they were last worn while driving from Carlisle to Birmingham and served their purpose to soak up the perspiration omitted from his crotch; she may have wanted to use that particular bra later, which is why it was strategically positioned on the back of the door, idiot!

Over time couples learn to live with each other, or learn to accept inadequacies and little traits. What a crock! Although this might be true for most couples the acceptance of these inadequacies is not always the case and little things that bug and niggle them soon grow into bigger niggles that cause constant nagging as one tries to change the other; this is the essence of relationships and where 'nagging' is defined.

In homemaking simple things such as picking up pants, taking an empty coffee cup from the lounge into the kitchen, washing up, loading and unloading the dishwasher, hanging the washing out and even cutting the lawn (see the first book if you like) if not done when expected lead to wonderful little comments that men decipher as 'nagging' when they are said as 'requests and reminders' by a woman. Why? For the solitary reason that women think men cannot remember to do simple things on their own and they need reminding to keep them on their toes. That's it; without doubt men are thick, are incapable of making the right choices and don't remember anything!

What women don't realise is that men work on the principle of 'just in time' and we do remember that certain things need to be done but if it can be done a little later then that is completely acceptable to us. After all as long as 'it' is done then what is the problem? Flapping about stuff is unhealthy! This foolish approach is going to cause a comment or two, just like these ones.

I've asked you, I don't know how many times already!

"Yes I know you have, but I wanted to make sure that I understood completely first, honey"

The second and third request has nothing to do with a man's perception that the job actually isn't life threatening and so delaying the job is perfectly normal. Unacceptable, but normal in his eyes but not in the eyes of a woman; actually this reluctance demonstrates a churlish trait that really annoys women and as the standoff continues to boil up the chances of it becoming a real issue increases.

You never do anything

"Oh thanks, I'm always doing shitty stuff, how rude!"

Rude or not, the impression is that if a man doesn't do one thing, then they have never done anything, ever! This type of criticism can only lead to one of two reactions, the first is an argument and an exchange of comments to score points, or secondly the now brow beaten bloke chunters off to finally do the job. Just do it in the first place!

The opinion that the lazy git never does anything is a common one for the vast majority of women and is certainly discussed on girlie nights out, "ooh I know, mine never does anything either, I ask him, but it makes no difference." This common opinion between the girls can therefore escalate with the security that her pals agree with her, because they have the same problem with their bloke. This heightened confidence can certainly add to the next barrage, when the man fails to do anything again. This leads on quite nicely to the next phrase.

Your just like all the others, a lazy arsehole

"You mean the hubbies of your mates or the other blokes you have downtrodden before?"

By the way what is a 'lazy arsehole'? Is it one that is lazy and has an arse or is it one with a problem with their sphincter muscle and thus has serious problems controlling their bowels.

Either way I have never really understood this abusive phrase as a constructive one, other than breaking it down to lazy and bum hole. Charming, whoops I used one of their words, but the same applies as we can again translate charming into 'b*stard, or alternatively 'b*tch' this time instead.

I don't know why I bother!
"Nor do I, but that's another opinion that will fall on deaf ears"

In most cases this little beauty is the last thing said and is said as a woman walks off, in the hope that the guilt trip thrust upon her man will encourage him to actually do the job requested.

Family Ties

What happens behind closed doors is one thing but what happens at a family gathering is another. Much the same as a social event at work or with friend's women and men adopt different persona's and this on its own can really annoy their partner.

In a family environment this alien persona is often worse than at the friendly gathering. Is it down to showing the parents that she is independent and doesn't take any crap? It could be that a newly wed or even veteran wife wants to show her dominating parents of old that she has strength and doesn't need them anymore, well not in the same way.

Bravado creeps in and silly things are said that lead to 'public nagging' as well as 'private nagging' later at home. Men get cocky, especially if they are usually the life and soul of any party. Thus they can adopt a confident yet arrogant persona while yearning for a little bit of respect from his in-laws who still feel that their little princess has sold out for a less than average hubby.

Take the various holidays, such as Christmas and Easter, occasions when a couple take a turn at hosting the turkey-roasting bonanza. Parents and siblings arrive at the allocated time expectant of a fine meal and to be waited on for the day, plied with alcohol and leftovers for tea.

Before arriving couples franticly prepare the meal colliding physically as well as emotionally due to the pressure of the expectation to table a meal that the mother in law will accept as adequate. If one or other takes the head chef role in the kitchen then the other will assume the kitchen assistant or skivvy role. Not... even if the man is the accomplished cook his skivvy will no doubt question everything all morning.

Is everything under control? Sure?

"Yes it's sorted and yes I'm bloody sure"

A need for reassurance it may be, that the turkey isn't going to be overcooked or that chef hasn't forgotten to put the roast potatoes in, however asking every five minutes starts to grind, after the first thirty minutes!

There is probably a well thought out system, with a list of what goes in at what time; 10.30am Turkey in, 1.00pm Turkey out, Noon Spuds (parboiled at11.45am) into goose fat... simple!

On the subject of cooks and their kitchen we all know how volatile it can be, take Gordon Ramsay and his professional kitchen set up and the lambasting people get there, surely this is a justification for a man to be an arse in his own home, isn't it?

You need me to do anything?

"Actually yes, stop flipping asking if I need help, probably best if you go and do, I dunno, your nails"

Harsh, I know but again if this is the third time the question has been asked this past quarter of an hour it probably hasn't changed one iota.

Notwithstanding these comments, usually said with the best intentions, but said due to the pressure of the forthcoming day, the real opportunity to fall out comes when the guests arrive.

From the moment the mother in law arrives with a home made trifle, a bag of Satsuma's, a box of Quality Street and home made mince pies in a Tupperware box, any reaction to her plonking everything on the work surface is likely to receive daggers. After taking the 'working space' from the flustered chef she might even ask if she can help too. Oh Christ, stereo!

Ushering guests out of the kitchen might seem like a good idea but it is a dangerous move that is definitely going to cause a second look for being fricken rude, so it is probably best to let guests do their thing and mull around the kitchen until they get the hint that they are not going to get anywhere near the preparation and cause chaos.

Preparing the festive meal, perhaps for the first time, amounts to one thing. 'Comparison'. Mothers will compare the gravy, let's say, and if one mother likes the thick stuff with copious amounts of corn flour and Crosse & Blackwell Gravy Browning used in her secret recipe while the other always makes the light brown watery type then it provides a quandary for the couple, mums gravy or mums gravy? Even this can cause a problem, crazy isn't it? Oh just go half-way and have a mid brown version to keep the peace. Better still buy in the ready made stuff and heat it in the microwave...maybe not on reflection as it would cause problems and even worse the mothers might both then disappear into the kitchen to cross spatulas and cook up some palatable gravy to replace the tepid tasteless one from a plastic tub, with reduced salt.

As all accomplished cooks know the last half an hour is the critical time; the business end of any meal preparation to get everything ready at the right time. Rest the roast and carve the meat, to ensure the vegetables are served hot but not over mushy. So why is this the time that the cook is expected to break off from the final preparation and socialise with a glass of bucks fizz? Because it's a prerequisite, that's why.

Toasting the day with a glass in hand and smiling sweetly is what grown up kids have to do at family gatherings, for sure, and if presents are brought out it is only polite to sit and do the right thing, sod the meal and let the veg boil dry!

With an acceptable meal served, the rest of the day is like walking on eggshells for many a man, making sure that he doesn't come out with a sarcastic comment in his attempt to inject some fun into the day. If he does then he can expect a comment or two.

Don't speak to my parents like that!

"But I was only kidding, where's your sense of humour?" Usually said to a man at the end of a long day, but occasionally after a few short minutes. It can be a bit of banter, in his opinion, about the mother in laws pressie, you know the spa day voucher, however saying it isn't a miracle in an envelope probably isn't the right thing to utter. The expensive bottle of red given to dad maybe not Rioja, his favourite, but it is a good bottle of wine anyway and suggesting he doesn't neck it like he normally does is another catalyst for this defensive comment on behalf of a woman's parents.

Have you said thank you for your present

"What? Am I six years old here, yes I have but should I now write a thank you note now and on the floral notepaper my mother has given me as a stocking filler?" Never mind the sycophantic thank you that was said while the veg was boiling dry and that was obviously missed, being asked, nay getting told to say it again just in case they missed it first time around is acceptable.

Other family members attending the celebrations can cause a bit of friction, the sister in law that never reciprocates the hosting of the annual get together and is content to come year after year to someone else's place to eat drink and try and get merry.

The brother in law who sits on his arse and in the comfy chair to the point that he could have conceivably died and no one would have noticed until 'phew', a right arm is raised and the glass in his hand is waved in attempt to get a refill from the host. It would be nice if he brought a few cans with him but that is too much to expect. This display of draconian manhood at work however never gets him any 'nag pie' the pikey-lowlife!

Still knowing the family politics anything said would probably fall on deaf ears anyway.

Making a suggestion that the brother in law actually has the ability to get off his arse and fill his own glass with the free booze might be what everyone is thinking but saying it out loud can leave our host in deep water, "you know how difficult it is for my sister, show some respect" is whispered, or shouted in the kitchen. Balls to em both, always on the beg!

Other family gatherings are weddings, birthday bashes and funerals; each with definitive rules for any outspoken man; keep his gob shut and resist the temptation to even make farting noises with his mouth when someone bends over. A man must be on his guard when surrounded by family members and should always avoid reacting to any derogatory comment about his job, house or car. Any comment made about his wife is a 'get out of jail free card' and he is then allowed to defend his wife with a chivalrous act. Perfectly acceptable...as long as he doesn't go too far and embarrass her by front snap kicking the big fat gypo before knocking him out with well timed 'Doo Jirugi', that's a double punch for all non Taekwon-Do readers!

Growing Older...Perfecting the Home

The chapter is about homemaking and besides the open house policy for friends and family the gradual evolution of a couple improving the abode with regular DIY and maintaining the cleanliness, which leads to those regular little slices of 'nag pie' covered earlier and in the first book, the evolution and perfecting of the art of 'nagging' is the next phase for any woman.

We all have agendas in life, things that we want to do, material objects we would like and for the vast majority of couples, adding to the fold. Deciding to try for a baby is a joyous decision and one that can bond a couple with a common goal, get pregnant and have a trouble free pregnancy. It does however generate a bit of friction if it doesn't happen straight away, is a man firing on all cylinders? Are his drinking or other habits stopping his little fishes work properly or are they lethargic, just as he is in life?

Getting pregnant becomes a project for many women after a couple of months; all of a sudden certain dietary requirements are introduced and from a steak and chips, rice and dairy are introduced to boost the production of the vital juice of life. Normal things done every week are forbidden in the schedule, in case they slow the tadpoles down. The monthly clock is put up on the wall and the optimum time to 'do it' is highlighted in yellow, if it coincides with a regular night out with the lads so be it!

This might seem a bit regimented and tongue in cheek it is an extreme example but let us face it, at least it is a time when a bloke gets his oats regularly and after doing the deed to the best of his ability, he is safe, in the happy knowledge that he won't have to use a valuable 'shag me on presentation voucher', that he received for his birthday, tomorrow because the wall planner has taken the spontaneity out of the love making. The book of vouchers remains intact and can be saved for another day, hopefully before the expiry date of 2020 though. Shouldn't be a problem though as there are only five vouchers in the booklet. Which reminds me I found three unused ones in my everything drawer, wonder if they are still valid and worth cashing in, or would that be wrong now?

You won't find a man complaining here about lack of horizontal pleasures at this energetic time, oh no. He will more likely complain how bleeding knackered he is with it all. However knowing his luck it will last a month at best and after planting his seed her legs will close up like the Thames Tidal Barrier at extreme high tide! The press-stud will be stitched in again and the haberdashery department will make a sale of some more Velcro. After all once pregnant it would be wrong to scare the embryo with that 'thing' coming towards it like a torpedo from the darkest depths, poor little thing.

After getting past the dangerous stage and when the announcement is made to the parents that they are going to be classed as grand old people now, the focus eventually moves to preparing the nursery and buying prams, car seats, clothes, a bottle steriliser and all of a sudden the credit card takes a bashing from the purchases. Does it matter? No it's great. The nine months of bliss do come with the dreaded hormone imbalance and psychological downers about the change in a woman's body. These in turn can lead to some left field comments that some would describe as 'nagging' but others would term as 'a cry for help and reassurance' either way they can make a man feel stuck in no mans land.

Oh I look like a beach ball
"Yes you do, but a sexy beach ball"

Whatever a man says it will come out wrong or be heard as the wrong thing to say. The word 'glowing' is the best one to use for any bloke, 'radiant' is another but agreeing with the beach ball description is not the right thing to say.

Do you still fancy me?
"Of course darling, would you like a cuddle or maybe something else to prove that I do? My bad the torpedo might scare Zoggy, a cuddle it is then"

Here's the thing the woman is carrying his child and of course he loves and fancies her but in her 'no access phase' a bit of doubt is going to creep in that he isn't going off her and looking at other women. Where does it come from? Stories at the antenatal class from the one woman whose husband has been playing away for years, great, they all now doubt their hubbies.

I Want!
The demands of any woman range from donuts at 10pm, mild, to the latest Mamas and Papas pram, to replace the one already bought in anticipation of the new arrival, severe!

Any contra opinion is often greeted by the famous phrase, "All I am asking for is one thing, after all I am carrying your child, it's the least you can do!"

The extreme demand is for a new house or an

extension because there is no way that a family of three or four will function in the three-bedroom semi. So with a comfortable and affordable existence home-making changes from the current house to a bigger one and until they agree on what she wants there will be a chance that they will differ on the point. For the vast majority of couples the feasibility of moving and taking on a bigger mortgage is not an option anyway, especially if he hasn't fulfilled his potential and been promoted over the short years they have been together. Now if they are on benefits and enjoy rent-free accommodation courtesy of the taxpayer then it won't be his problem but one for the council worker who has to find a suitable house to fit the brood of six kids, with more to follow as soon as the caesarean scar heals up. Why work when you can earn more from the taxpayer, it's far easier to breed kids and spend the money on ear piercing and number one haircuts!

Don't get me wrong these are not commonplace wish list items for women, but I am pretty sure that they will ring true for a few readers of this section of the book, perhaps with a variance on the actual want but with the same kind of reaction from men and women alike.

'Going with the flow' is a great phrase and in all seriousness as long as the new arrival is healthy and has a place to be loved, fed, changed and watered, isn't that enough for any couple?

Here I go again getting a tad more serious on what is actually a satirical book on the things women say to men and what men say to women. It isn't being melancholy at all but amidst the funny side of the subject matter there is a need to recognise that not every relationship is as harsh as I am making out. The balance to the very tongue in cheek opinions and observations made also have a very serious side that any psychologist or psychiatrist would see beneath the veil of humour and there are many heart-wrenching observations that can be spotted in any relationship as the first signs or reasons for marital breakdown. In some ways this attempt to make it sound funny is to demonstrate how ridiculous 'nagging' is and how it can lead to real anguish.

But enough of the disclaimer, again a reminder that I am not a psychologist, by definition, just someone who like many of us recognises the waste of life that we humans demonstrate by analysing everything and reading what we want out of our analysis. In a man's view, or case, it is deciding that it simply 'nagging', from those wonderful comments!

Through this analysis we hope to improve and this is the crux of the book, the different ages of a woman and her perfecting what men class as nagging. Living with a partner goes one of two ways, acceptance of those inadequacies or a gradual increase in the intensity and discontent as a partner becomes immune to the same comments over time, therefore to make a point the severity of the criticism increases.

But now for something completely different; still a part of life that couples and families share for a few short weeks every year, the vacation.

4
Vacations

For a week, maybe two or in some cases quite a few weeks in the year a trip overseas or in this country are regarded as perfect times for couples and families to spend with each other.

Waking up to glorious sunshine and spending all day doing stuff together is quality time that can create memories that will last a lifetime. It can mean another set of memories, I think you know where I am going with this one don't you?

The fact that a couple and a family are thrust to-gether, in a family room 24/7, is much different to the zones that are clearly defined at home. Daughters have their room, father has the Sky+ controller in the snug or lounge and mother lays claim to the bath-room and bedroom. If father works away from home for lengthy periods then mum and daughter may even have a two-zone philosophy during the week. Ying and Yang prevails and all is well.

It shouldn't matter then that for two weeks the zone system is abolished and indeed the relish of leisure, not work, for either mum or dad is what they work for the rest of the year.

Why is it then that vacation time is a recipe for disaster for some families? By the way I am referring to vacation time instead of holidays? Simply because

'The Holidays' refers to Christmas for our American readers, who by the way will probably not recognise two weeks as a real vacation because they are lucky to get more than a week off a year, bless them.

This Chapter is therefore a journey within our journey through the 'Life of Pie' a story within a story, and on that note, let me begin.

From the moment the alarm goes off on the morning of the outbound flight the potential for 'nagging' and bickering starts. Actually no, it probably starts days before when the packing phase is underway. Men can't help get frustrated when the suitcases are packed to the brim with lotion, toiletries and more matching sets of underwear than days overnight. Trying to close the case is always a problem and especially when the lock snags on one of the dozen pairs of shoes that have been strategically placed around the edges.

Any suggestion to perhaps, "take a few pairs out" is treated with contempt, especially if the selection of footwear is clearly included to match up with a particular dress that is planned for one of the nights at the resort, how stupid are men, pah?

When it comes to closing the suitcases, finally, the next task is to weigh them on the bathroom scales to see if they are 'legal' or run the risk of excess baggage charges. If by chance they, or at least one, are over the baggage allowance the next step is to open the whole lot and then move stuff from one case to another to spread the load and then attempt to close them up again. All good if they the pass the bathroom scale test, but be aware of the possible embarrassment at the check in counter if the bathroom scales have been wound down by a few pounds so that when a woman weighs herself the readout is acceptable, not the true reading!

If the now balanced suitcases are still over then

there is only one option and one that is sparked by this next classic phrase.

Well, take some of your stuff out

"Oh great, I have two pairs of shoes, well one for the posh restaurant and a pair of trainers – plenty but perhaps I should take one shoe of each out, would that help?"

Fourteen nights equates to half a dozen pairs of boxer shorts, six t-shirts, a couple of summer shirts, one pair of long trousers and three pairs of shorts. Total space required, a quarter of a suitcase, but with one ingenious extra item, the 'holiday wash kit', basically soap powder in a compact packet, brilliant!

There is an option to save more space and nominal extra weight to actually take the 'holiday wash kit' out, of course, and use the onsite laundry spotted in the brochure, or even the laundry service provided by housekeeping.

This is solution will not only save 250 grams but justify the request to halve the number of his clothes taken anyway, especially if the intention is to wash out items part way into the vacation already, "well if you are going to launder your clothes you don't need as many anyway!" The alternative to washing undies through is to go commando on a few nights, but caution is needed here if the baggy shorts are the only ones that win a place in the case, meat and veg on display can upset small children and people sitting opposite in a restaurant or bar, no matter how good their eyesight is!

Another potential problem is if the room air conditioning is turned to low, then washing out items will be flawed if the items don't dry overnight. A balcony and tropical evenings however belay this observation.

With debate comes opinion, with opinion comes disagreement, with disagreement comes frustration,
with frustration comes analysis, with analysis comes
observation, with observation comes comment...

Why do you get so wound up?

*"Ooh, let me think, because I would like to relax and start
enjoying the fact that we are on out holibobs but you now
want to recheck the suitcases, tickets and passports for the
third time. If we haven't brought it we will buy it...jeez!"*
With a six o'clock alarm set, packing the suitcases
again at 1.37am is a recipe for disaster in the morning.
Now 'Grumpy' might be one of the characters that the
family hopes to see while in Florida, but it stands a
chance that Grumpy will be here too in less than five
hours. The problem in hand is to get the cases closed
and here the use of a small child to sit on the top is a
good idea; or use the 'principal packer' resisting the
temptation to get her to put her fingers in and push
the protruding bra strap back in and letting the lid
close by accident! Grumpy can wait for now with the
mission to close the suitcases accomplished, for now.

Fitting everything into suitcases, however, is a
problem compounded by the inclusion of kids clothes
and a kid's suitcase. Again the same rules apply to
multiple knickers, vests, shoes, Jellies, Crocs and
tops even though it stands a chance that three or four
items will be worn throughout the two-week adventure. After all why would a daughter wear a pair of
shoes that she doesn't like or make her feet sore in a
foreign country if she wont wear them at home. The
lack of space in the cases is alleviated by taking a kids
suitcase a pink one that has a little space for clothes
but primarily contains a selection of cuddly toys that
have to be taken, because it isn't fair to leave them

behind. Unfortunately a small pink suitcase from Tesco designed as hand luggage might fail the check in criteria and end up in the aircraft hold and thus at the mercy of the Neanderthal baggage handler at the destination airport, and so soft toys are actually a good call.

Pre-Flight Ironing

There is one more little observation that causes a few differing opinions during the packing phase of the vacation experience. Ironing clothes! Okay a once over is acceptable but spending three hours removing every crease from every item and laying them per-fectly in the suitcase. What in heavens name is that all about? No matter how many holidays I have been on, including business trips overseas and many an overnight stay in a hotel, I have never unpacked an item without at least one crease, even after using IQ to alleviate the problem by 'rolling items'. A long haul flight means that clothes will be creased, it is a proven fact and a foregone conclusion that baggage leaves a passengers protection and ends up on a trailer, piled high, and is thus subject to pressure from cases on top and a touch of gravity if at the bottom of the pile. Once chucked, kicked and stepped on while entering the aircrafts baggage hold it is then subject to cabin decompression which in turn sucks the damn air out of the baggage hold and guess what? Yes compressed and creased clothes too, with the added bonus of sun tan lotion that has found it's way out of the bottle onto his clothes. Suitcase leaks always end up on a man's clothes don't they, not hers, why? Because a woman strategically packs her clothes away from liquid items and uses his socks and trunks to wrap the liquid items.

So, why in the name of Jetsteam Irons do women

start ironing at 11pm the night before the flight and take particular care over each item? Just bosh the iron over it and chuck it in, then repair the creases at the other end, if you can be arsed; that is what the travel iron is for!

Turn That Bloody Alarm Off!

With the trauma of packing a mere memory, when the alarm goes off, the excitement should be at its peak... shouldn't it? Hopefully but early morning starts and a late night before are ingredients for a few crossed words, especially if the suitcases are unlocked and opened again to put the toothbrushes in!

Checking the plug points is essential to avoid a fire while away, according to the mother in law that is. Never mind the fact that the same sockets are on for 48 weeks of the year, vacation time when clearly the fire risk is greater when the item is plugged in but not being used and generating amps. Therefore turning off the kettle, electric fan oven and television not only save 'stand by' electricity but help prevent a possible inferno. But if certain sockets are chucked off before the hair straighteners have been used, a man can expect a rollocking if they are still cold when required! "Oh for god's sake I thought my electric Head Gear ones were on and warming up, now I'm going to have to get the GHD butane ones out of the suitcase!" and so the cases are unlocked and opened again. Just to make a point no doubt.

After the final 'socket check' the next thing is to close the suitcases for the last time and then put the identifying strap and sticker on them, spin the combination and attempt to get 30 kilos of dead weight downstairs, without taking a chunk out of the wall plaster on the stairs. Receiving a piece of advice from the top of the stairs such as, "careful, mind the walls, take your time now!" isn't helpful by the way. Speed is sometimes inevitable with such a weight and the Laws of Perpetual Motion, indeed the wall might be the friction element here!

Let's Go!

If the taxi is waiting the final bit of frustration for any man that wants to get going is when a woman decides to write a note for her parents, who are kindly checking the post and house every day for the duration of the vacation. Why this note wasn't scribed straight after finishing the ironing at midnight is a question that enters the logic argument? If a man says anything he will be accused of being ungrateful that her parents have been 'kind enough' to keep an eye on the house. Ungrateful it may be but any bloke knows that the house will be fine without it's occupants, not lonely at all, and even if there is an almighty leak or another disaster, the presence of his in-laws will not make any difference to an insurance claim. The security factor is also important, yes, and it is accepted that a thief will know if a family is away if the post is piled up in the porch, but the solid door has a way of hiding the build up. Nevertheless, on return at least they can expect a pile of junk mail on the kitchen work surface and a neat pile of free newspapers and serious post, oh and a loaf of bread, pint of milk and packed of bacon in the otherwise empty fridge. Let's hope that the burglar doesn't look through the kitchen window shall we!

Note written, the house can be secured and whether taking a taxi or the family car, the sigh of relief is a loud one for everyone as the next stop is the airport. If the family car is used then long stay parking means a further stop off and with only a few short hours sleep, lugging cases out of the car, onto the transit bus and back off again can really sap energy levels. A bit of help is always welcome but if the small child is in tow, pulling her own lightweight pink suitcase and the wife is busy last minute texting work or a friend then a man can expect to have to take charge of two or three bags. Not wanting to spend £5 hiring a trolley to go 300 metres to the check in desk, he will therefore try and roll the suitcases carefully, hoping that they don't topple over and rip his shoulder out, thus dislodging the carefully balanced holdall that keeps swinging forward and hitting his elbow. Very annoying that, isn't it!

Check In

Arriving later than anticipated and facing a queue of 200 people in front is occasionally the last straw for a now knackered bloke. Beads of sweat rolling down his temples and toys now thrown out of the pram; blame is sought to vent frustration. The likely suspect is therefore always going to be the wife, who cost them five minutes writing the note and another five insisting he double check the socket she might have turned on as a back up for Head Gear straighteners, or the iron that she used quickly to smuggle a couple of extra sun tops into the suitcases while he was turning the sockets off upstairs, What was actually turned off in the end? Who knows now!

These little delays have likely cost them a hundred places in the queue and that means less time to chill out in the departure lounge. Grumpy has entered the departure area and yes, typecasting means that it is dad who is the newest cast member.

It is a dangerous time for Grumpy; he has to keep it all together so that the security guy doesn't get the hump at his attitude. As the stern looking uniformed employee wheels the laptop on a plinth slowly up the waiting line, checking tickets and passports to save a few minutes at the actual check in, if Grumpy gives out a bit of attitude he faces a bag inspection on the spot or worse a body cavity search, and so smiling sweetly is the best option.

At check in the pre-booked seats is a godsend and the only chance for any disagreement is if the suitcases are overweight. If they are then the worst thing that Grumpy can hear his better half say to the check in lady is, "Didn't I say you had too much in there, I'm so sorry, just charge the excess fee." Brilliant with inclusion of spare clothes, shoes, medications and Aloe Vera travel shampoo they are now £50 lighter and they haven't even had a nice cup of coffee yet!

Departure Imminent – Last & Final Call

A bit of an extreme example of what can happen, but how close is it to you reading this? Opportunities will present themselves for a bit of 'nagging' after check in and throughout the long flight ahead.

Duty free is another chance to engage in a woman's favourite pastime, shopping for bargains.

Another bottle of perfume "oooh VAT free", a pair of sunglasses to compliment the Gucci handbag, even a new travel iron and spare travel adapters, in case the ones in the suitcase don't work at the other end. If a man voices any concern over non-essential yet 'too good to be true' purchases then he runs the risk of being labelled cheap and still playing the Grumpy character, so best to let the spree unfold.

While this spree does unfold the job in hand is to keep a keen eye on the departure board. This is a perfect job for kids, sending them off on the adventure every five minutes to check on the gate call, thus relieving the boredom for them. It is a good idea to check their progress to make sure the gate call hasn't been missed, after all there is nothing worse than hearing "passengers Gibson times three this is the last and final call for flight CO27 to Newark" over the muffled and rather loud Tannoy.

Once on board the spree might continue with a look at the in-flight shop items that are available, especially if the second bottle of perfume or Touché éclat is on offer. The limited stock on-board is something that might stem the flow of holiday cash into the pursers pouch and limit yet more bags to carry through customs and passport control at the destination.

Apart from the occasional delay or the missed flight window because another family were late embarking the only other stress factor is the possibility of very annoying kids in the row behind, perhaps the family that was late boarding. If the seats were pre-booked then it will be a man's fault if he has booked next to the family with matching England kits, including new tracksuit bottoms. The family from hell, no manners, no discipline and if anyone dares question them they run the risk being 'offered out' at 30,000 feet by another Grumpy cast member. This one has tattoos, not one of Snow White by the way, and he is really on edge after three pints of lager at the departure lounge bar before breakfast and nicotine deficiency brought on by the self-inflicted further delay because his brood were late to the gate. His last fix was when sucking on a roll up just before checking in, some six hours ago! Indeed the last time he went six hours without a fag he was 13, and that includes nighttime when he always wakes up for a smoke around 3am, washed down with a swig of Stella!

Arrivals

After a long flight and making new friends with the nice family that sat squabbling behind you for twelve hours, when the plane taxi's to the arrival gate why does this cause a stampede as soon as it comes to rest? People jockey for position as soon as the plane stops, jumping out their seats unaware that there is a ten minute wait while the doors are cross checked and the First Class, Premium Economy passengers and the wheelchair passenger in row seven, who has a connecting flight, are let off first. Mere mortal passengers in cattle class end up crushed and dodge baggage taken out of overhead lockers, crowding the aisles while others attempt to stand up cramped from waist height in the window seats their shoulders and heads inadvertently turning reading lights on and off and calling the hostess via the orange button! Just sit down and wait, after all the anticipation of a huge queue at passport control is next. Clearing passport control and customs, a really fun experience after all!

If it is Florida or a country that requires green visa waiver forms, then they better be filled in properly otherwise it is back to the end of the queue to fill the form out properly. If a man takes charge of this form filling then it will be his fault if they are rejected by the Homeland Security Official. More waiting and aching shoulders from the hand luggage is nothing compared to the plastic bags from the duty free spree that cut the circulation off in the fingers. This is another problem if the finger print scanner can't make out the digit when the blood rushes into the finger tips and bloats the image so that it nearly matches a wanted al-Qaida suspect from the 'Deck of Cards'.

Once through passport control and resisting the temptation to engage in a witty conversation with the official looking person who has either had far too much Botox or is genuinely devoid of facial expression to match the personality level, the final arrival experience is to collect the baggage from the carousel. With many hundreds of people surrounding the winding belt, space is at a premium and whole families take a place instead of a 'nominated luggage claimant' that can pass the recovered bags backwards to the waiting wife that is guarding the trolley and children, while texting her mum to say that 'we have all arrived safely, mwah x, PS, can you check that the iron was unplugged wen u pop round, thx x." This important message is of course only possible if the phone has been registered for overseas use and if so the signal is found and the mobile registers to AT&T or T-Mobile at £1 a text! If not a request to use the man's work phone is the only option available, let's hope that there aren't any cryptic messages that ping up, but that comes in a later Chapter!

Small children run the risk of losing a finger as they can't help but touch the belt on the carousel and a second risk of being cracked on the head by a fast moving suitcase grabbed by a burly bloke just before it passes for another circuit. We have all seen it a Samsonite whipped the off just in time, after checking with his wife that "Carmen...luv...this is one of ours, innit?" It is so dangerous for anyone in range of the projectile and so why do parents let six year olds stand next to them at the baggage reclaim? This observation is repeated in baggage claim halls all over the planet every day and if anyone raises an eyebrow or passes a comment then they risk being 'offered out' by the bloke in the England top who clearly doesn't give a shit whether his kid ends up a digit down. He is on holiday and is now desperate for a fag, anyone that gets in the way or glances at his kid or indeed his kids number one haircut with the long bit left around the nape, is cruising for a bruising. This threat means anyone, even the 90 year old war hero now in a wheelchair, nobody is safe, apart from the security crew who could do everyone a favour and 'double tap' a couple of rounds into his chest that is! Sorry, I digressed again.

Sods Law dictates that if you have three suitcases in the baggage hold then two will be on the first pass and the third, probably the pink one, will be right at the end. So, with only a dozen or so people left the last suitcase rolls around can finally be reunited with the family. At last!

Coach or Car?

After the baggage claim the next mission is to collect a hire car or find the resort bound bus, which means having to, once again, walk from the terminal to the hire desk or bus stop to face more queues. This is a recipe for the first cocktail of the holibobs, well a Molotov cocktail if a smidgen of criticism is made about how far away the next mini destination is. Especially if the bloke booked with Hertz instead of Enterprise and Hertz is half a mile away in another terminal. Idiot!

When hiring a family car in advance it can save a few quid but the representative will always try and upsell to a soft-top or SUV, for "only a few dollars." This pitch is perfectly timed, after 14 hours of traveling and suitcase humping, a sales pitch timed so that tired and weary gullible travelers are at their lowest resistance and agree to an upgrade. If however Mr Grumpy doesn't want to spend any more money and is 'short' with the hire car representative then Mrs Grumpy can get a tad annoyed with his attitude and low and behold the first argument on foreign soil starts, "you are so rude to people, it is so embarrassing, you have been an arsehole all day!" Probably right but I wonder why!

For the travelers that are on the resort bound coach this can mean a two hour trip dropping off at every other hotel before arriving at their hotel destination, a trip that would take 40 minutes by car. This observation will no doubt be voiced if he was adamant that a hire car was a waste of money when they booked the vacation all those months ago.

SUV upgrade accepted, to avoid the embarrassment and the extra dollars taken from Amex, finally it is off to the toll road and onward to 'destination hotel'.

For the independent travelers, the next phase is to negotiate the exit signs, find the expressway and remember to drive on the other side of the road. Any loss of concentration will result in a shriek and some advice on how to drive safely, not like a lunatic. If toll roads are used then a man better be prepared with some small foreign change to chuck into the bucket. Unfortunately expressway and turnpike tollbooths don't take travelers cheques and so even if he has secured some small value bills in advance let us hope that the in-flight shopping didn't mean using the small dollar bills instead of using the $100 bill instead.

Hotel Bliss

The map carefully followed, tolls thankfully paid without a detour to the Bank of America for change, SUV parked up, suitcases out and room allocated all mean one thing, the vacation has started. Time to open the crushed cases and unpack.

Opening the suitcases provides definitive proof

that the argument on creased clothes is won by the bloke as crushed items are taken out and hung on the hangers to let the creases 'drop out naturally' instead of ironing them again. A good call on purchasing a second travel iron! Thankfully with only a few of the husbands items that made the final packing manifest at home this doesn't compromise the hanging space required for his wife, especially as there are only five hangers in the wardrobe.

All this unpacking however assumes that the room allocated is acceptable and is roach free has an aroma of Lavender and not Lambert and Butler. This is one of those moments when a man is silently tested on what is acceptable. If, historically he has been vocal about another substandard hotel room, very similar to the encounter with the car hire representative that caused huge embarrassment, then he has a tough choice to make if the room is a little sub standard. Reject it and storm off to the foyer to politely request a new room, or stay quiet and get another dressing down for accepting the crap room! Waiting for the wife to voice her concerns and then agree is probably the best option.

Room reallocated and indeed upgraded to a pool view, repacking and then unpacking the clothes once more leaves one final task for the day...Exploring the hotel. With a new lease of life after such a long trip, finding the eateries, pool and games room is mandatory and after a day of potential carnage. Yay! Family time has started in earnest.

The next twelve days, that is two weeks less a day traveling either end, are a mixture of fun packed activities, late nights and late starts. Being together 24/7 is a new experience and the combination of heat, alcohol, claustrophobic conditions and differing opinions on what to do every day are what we call the 'classic vacation'.

If time zones are the only zones of concern with space now at a premium for twelve days, then heading West-wards means waking up early until body clocks adjust and the alarm is needed to avoid missing breakfast. This isn't always the case for people that could sleep through a nuclear war and maybe on a 'bed of nails'. These people are the 'Bagpuss's' of modern times and waking them up early while on vacation is not a good idea, even if the rest of the brood are up and at it ready for the day. The golden rule of vacations is that everyone walks at the same pace as the slowest person in the group and they all have to leave the hotel room when the last person has woken up, put the P20 sunblock, let it dry, dressed and put the es-sential items in a suitable bag. These essential items include, regular sunblock, the small tube of Factor 50 for noses, Evian spray to cool the face down, a spare pair of flip flops, lip gloss, Kleenex tissues, Amex card, a spare top, spare tops for the kids, a pen and paper, mobile phone, cash and of course replacement nail varnish in case any chips off in the pool. Poor planning or waiting to see what the weather is doing might gen-erate a discussion on what the day holds for a family, probably over breakfast that is being eaten at 10.30, but that isn't important because they are on vacation and time is meaningless.

Fueled up and ready to go, the busy fun filled days soon mingle into a week with a trip here and a trip there. Further opportunity to catch up on some sleep by flaking out on a sunbed is bliss for Bagpuss.

It doesn't matter at all as long as everyone is happy and for a family a water park is perfect for everyone to do their own thing. The same can be said for the pool area at a hotel or the beach. Luxury and warmth, well, as long as the sun is out and it isn't raining. If it is raining then alternative plans will be needed or the purchase of ponchos and flip flops to sweat under and provide more items to launder in the room.

For every day spent in the sunshine there is the chance to eat together as a family, a rare occurrence at home if mum and dad work stupid hours and arrive home at sporadic times during the week. Eating out can be on the hoof or might involve going back to the room, showering changing and making an event of the planned meal. This in turn will probably involve one or more of the family unit sitting and waiting for the final member to get ready, change into the outfit that matches the shoes brought for the occasion or alternatively having a fashion display with opinion sought on which pair work best with the outfit. God forbid that the shoes are chosen but with an outfit change to compliment the preferred pair!

What does this all demonstrate? Men are impatient and are happy throw any old thing on, creased and all, as long as they can get out and eat, drink and soak up the atmosphere. The only difference here is when a vacation is for a couple, here the room is a place that a bloke wants to use and take advantage of the sunshine aphrodisiac that is in abundance. They want to spend as much time in, under the covers before dinner and back under again at the end of the evening's entertainment. With a family room these vacations are merely a distant memory and a good reason to get a one-bedroom condo next time, sod the extra cost!

I could add a few more examples in here but I would rather leave you to think about your own vacation experiences and remember the wonderful memories and, like me, cast any 'nagging' memories to the back of your mind. Actually writing this Chapter has given me an idea for another book, just about 'vacations', but then you would probably decide that I really am a moaning old git, which would be a fair assumption but actually off the mark. I loved family vacations, even though they posed a few hurdles for me and every other bloke probably. Today I relish the time I can holiday with my daughter, and with fond memories of past vacations, I now have the beauty of only coping with one woman who is more than happy to get up and go off to a theme park or water park and partake in breakfast before they stop serving and swap the menu over to lunch and a different fare.

This also presents us with the opportunity to sit back and titter at families that are obviously struggling to keep each other happy with the majority vote on the day's activities. Moaning kids, fathers on a short fuse and mothers having a go at fathers for telling the kids off…breakfast at Ponderosa with free entertainment. Can't beat it!

But enough of the psychoanalysis and specifically 'vacation nagging' and in turn the unmistakable effect that it has on individuals; let's consider the fun part again and move on to a specific Chapter that revolves around a recent innovation to most of us, the impact of technology and extension of 'face-to face nagging' via a cellular signal or in the 3G and EE world where we interact with each other through social media.

5
The Third Screen

Mobile Phones

One of the wonders that we have seen over the last couple of decades is the arrival of the mobile phone. Instead of using phones with wires to talk to people some genius woke up one morning and decided to develop one without wires.

Now this gadget has emerged from resembling a brick wired to a car battery into smart phones that have as much technology in the handy credit card sized ones we have today than used to put Armstrong and Aldrin on the moon; unless the moon landings didn't happen and the conspiracy theorists are right that it was filmed in downtown Houston, behind a Dunkin Donuts drive through.

For those of us that remember what it was like to actually be free and untraceable until we got home or to until we were contactable on a landline at work, then you will relate to the massive change that cell phone technology has had on a woman's ability to 'nag' from a distance.

Prior to mobile phones 'nagging' was reserved to face-to-face confrontation and or via the telephone. When having a phone became a necessity the text message and call options left no excuse for not under-standing what was expected of the recipient.

Mobiles allowed a message to be sent to bring a

pint of milk in on the way home from work, a reminder text not to forget and a voicemail to reinforce the texted question or request.

Partners could keep in touch 24/7, even from one continent to another if apart, and even if one is out socialising. Brilliant isn't it? Until couples realised that this was actually restrictive and maybe controlling at a new level. But let's not over analyse the implication of this technological advancement and merely state that with mobile phones very much part of life today that it also leaves no opportunity to ignore any obligation to do something.

The Chapter is about the third screen so I will therefore concentrate of the funny little comments that revolve around mobiles.

Forget the standard ringtones that used to drive people nuts in public places, you know the laser blast or bell ring copy of the old fashioned dial telephone, because we can now download 30-second snippets of favourite songs or badly recreated theme tunes or voiceover artists doing celebrity phrases. This has led to people having a ringtone for one contact and a different one for another to differentiate and warn who is calling before actually looking at the screen. This in turn has led to some songs that fit the caller beautifully such as the one I have for my mother, 'Maniac' by Michael Sembello; I know when I hear that little 160 beat per minute intro that it is an emergency because she is using her mobile phone. I am either in trouble or she needs picking up by Chris Cabs. I will also spill the beans on the one for a certain person that shall remain nameless, 'Everything She Want's' by Wham is particularly appropriate and you will relate to this if you know the lyrics and recognise that this classic track from George Michael and the other one is quite simply men's anthem to married life. The comparison for our women is of course 'I Will Survive' by Gloria Gaynor, which is probably my ringtone on some birds phone after dumping her abruptly, unless there is a song called 'asshole calling' that is, but break up's are covered later in the book.

New people added to the contact list might deserve a special ringtone; it might be a luvvy record that they first danced together to or a favourite 'Our Tune' that would still feature well on Simon Bates Radio Show. It might be a phased one depicting where the relationship is at a point in time such as 'I Can Do Better' by Avril Lavigne, or 'Boyfriend' by Bieber. Who knows, the possibilities are endless. Funny stories from friends can be used too to allocate that individual ringtone. One friend, stupidly once, referred to his wife's reluctance to partake in a certain sexual act, and his access to acceptable orifices were forcefully rejected. Quite right too as it is probably illegal in a few countries and US States! He was however allowed to approach the area with caution, touch but that's all. Straight after it seemed fairly appropriate to make 'Buffalo Gals' by Malcolm McLaren his ringtone, with the chorus part of the 30 second loop thus the lyrics "round the outside" emanating from my phone speaker when he called!

Other ringtones might be 'The Chinese Way' by Level 42 for that Asian contact or 'Mr Hate' by the Tubes for a horrible boss. Songs with peoples names in the title are a good option, 'Come on Eileen' by Dexy's Midnight Runners or 'Amy' by Greenday. However drawing the line at 'Fat Bottomed Girls' by Queen is probably appropriate; it's probably a thyroid related issue anyway.

Aside the plethora of ringtone options and the real

possibility that the contact will never ever hear the ringtone allocated because it's unlikely they will ever call you from the same room, the mobile phone can cause immense problems in a relationship, especially if the lock function is suddenly used or from a phone being left on the work surface in plain view it is all of a sudden never away from a sweaty palm or it gets taken into the shower, complete with a freezer zip bag to stop it getting wet, or is now taken to bed under the pillow at night.

Ever had that experience? If you have you will relate to this bizarre change in openness within a relationship. Of course it doesn't alter the requested access to your own phone, and with nothing to hide, why shouldn't it? Forget the times filling the car up and being careful not to have a phone next to the pump and so the Nokia was left in the car. Returning after collecting the loyalty points to find a woman trawling through text messages and call records, followed by...

*Who is 0**87 654321?*

"How the hell do I know, obviously not a contact otherwise I would have stored it, could be Countdown Cabs number, that fits!"

Is this a real number, god I hope not, hence the missing numbers just in case. Getting a third degree on a number is probably justified for naughty people but really is the trust that bad that every unallocated number of a call received instantly means something is fishy? Get a life!

If then further checks are made on the recent calls received or made tab and the same number appears more than once, then the fishy thingy is now a shoal of fish. "Why haven't you stored the person? Strange they must be important. Hmm?"

Why did you call her?

"Because she is my secretary and I needed to talk to her, didn't realise that I wasn't allowed to speak to an employee, silly me!"

If a woman uses that so-called 'sixth sense' that can evidently gauge when a man is lying or hiding something, then any unexplained or unusual call registered is an indication of something that doesn't add up.... hmm!

Is it wrong to have a co-workers number in your phone? Actually the unwritten rule is their business number is fine because they demonstrate the need to speak to a colleague out of hours, their private phone in the saved contacts in though is frowned upon by many a woman. Yes even in today's environment whereby people use these mobile phone thingies to communicate.

There is nothing worse though than receiving a call, a wrong number received at 10pm or a call from a colleague, especially a female one, by accident in her drunken state. Ever had that happen? I did and to this day no I have no idea why I got a call apart from the red faced apology on Monday morning and a demonstration of the contact list that had me next to her boyfriend, and the call made immediately afterwards to her chap to then correct the mistake. Not however that my casual explanation over dinner that evening belayed any concerns that it wasn't a freak call made in error. Women's intuition they call it! I would rather to refer to it as unfounded paranoia.

Itemised Phone Bills

A necessary tool for many company mobile users so that they can highlight personal calls and deduct them from monthly expense claim forms, however for a personal mobile their benefit is debatable in this day and age with inclusive minutes, data and text. Great to check the overseas call costs while say calling mother from Florida but apart from that getting a detailed itemised bill can cause a few problems, if left on the work surface, and a partner has the urge to check the calls herself. Spotting multiple calls to an unrecognised number can often instigate a call to Miss Marple in to investigate the observation. Miss Marple, in this instance, is probably her friend and the one who doesn't like men, Miss Andrist, not Miss Marple at all! If it is you can picture the conversation "There are ten calls to that number on the 12th?...... That was a Monday when he was overnight on business, peculiar isn't it, hmmm shall I ring it? with Miss Andrist replying, "Yes do it, find out who it is, catch the fecker out!"

Oh my god, a mind working overtime from a very insecure person is dangerous, if not a little pathetic and especially if the number is a customer, perhaps the person who was running late for a dinner meeting? Have you ever received a blocked call from a bloke or woman asking who you are? If you have it might be the wife or husband of someone you know who has spotted your number on an itemised bill, just saying!

SMS – Defn. 'Short Message Service' NOT 'Shag Me Senseless!'

Phone calls are one thing but text messages are in a league of their own when it comes to giving a plausible answer to any question about who, why and what for?

Text from? That's a bit strange?

Text messages from people cause just as much grief and it can become a bit crazy for a man or a woman if a work mate of the opposite sex texts late at night or at the weekend. Probably the best option, for our innocent ones, is to give the phone to the woman and just let her tell you what it says.... 'Hi soz but, It Okay if I get in later in the mo as I gotta b at dentist 4 9am, sore tooth'.... It also makes sense to let her keep the phone and ask her to reply for you so as to avoid the second question of what you said, dictate it by all means and hope that it is keyed in as dictated, "Yup c u wen u get in". No kiss should be dictated though, wholly inappropriate and indeed a full stop should be used to show a serious side and disgust at the intrusion on family time!

This open approach is how it should be, but is it though, does it work both ways? Does it hell, access to a blokes mobile phone is mandatory but question- ing a woman is an invasion of privacy. There are no grounds for questioning a kiss or wink on a text sent by her to him, oh no, that's what she does to everyone, and sometimes an emoji to lighten the mood. So what if she receives a dozen text messages in an hour and six are from a him, that bloke she never talks about when mentioning everyone else in the open plan office, it isn't grounds for any questioning; the same ques- tioning a man would get. What also happens is that the message alert will be left on to let a man know another one has come through, bing bong. Hmmm, even though engrossed in a television programme is the phone not on silent to make him wonder whether it is one of the girls or the hyperactive work colleague? What does he do? Ask, as she would, or ignore it because she wants him to ask? Ignore it and ignore subsequent messages that come through because it is none of his business is probably the best option. If this is the option then he will have to ignore the false laugh's and other messages that are greeted with a smile or titter, it's part of the game to keep a man on his toes? No explanation needed!

We all probably spend far too much time linking with friends and workmates on mobile phones rather than turning the bloody thing off and linking with partners. Is it boredom with home life or an addiction? I have never understood, for example, why people go on holiday and spend a fortune texting from overseas to the work 'friendship group' it doesn't make any sense at all to go on say a skiing trip and spend the evening texting the work group instead of enjoying the after ski entertainment in Val d'Isère. Step away from the phone and have a brandy hot chocolate or ten.

Now if a man's phone pings in between the text tennis correspondence that a woman is heavily involved, it is completely normal to get asked, "who's that from?" Equality my arse, or is that arsehole, the lazy one!

Selective privacy is probably the best way to describe access to a partner's mobile phone, maybe it is absolutely right to have a bastion of privacy, something that really doesn't need explaining at all, if there is trust. Although this makes perfect sense surely it's got to be an even playing field? Not a chance in hell!

Another phenomena that is a potential hot potato is the ability to track someone's phone, a great idea for security and now available to Joe Public after seeing how the intelligence services use GPS on shows like NCIS. Not such a great idea if the bleeping dot that the hundreds of 'Apps' available today show to narrow the location of the tracked mobile to within a few inches. Thus where the phone is defines where the owner is on a night out. It boils down to telling

the truth, not hiding anything, but for the less trusting partner using GPS tracking is just sad. If a man
goes out and after the curfew a woman decides to see
where he is, he had better not be in the Honey Club!
If he is then the next morning could go something like
this...

Where did you end up last night then?
"A few beers and then a curry"

Bearing in mind his phone was located on the High
Street, unless the curry house is upstairs and above
the downstairs lap-dancing bar, he is a bloody liar!
Even worse if, after being spotted by one of her friends
staggering into the pleasure pen last time he didn't
admit it and was copped lying, thus his faithful promise not to go again is another fib. Not that there is
anything wrong with engaging in conversation with
a Latvian beauty who's sole intent is to relieve him of
his hard earned dosh in return for a bit of bump and
grind. If that is his thing then so be it, but be honest
or face the undeniable evidence courtesy of a satellite
or two up above.

The same goes for the little green monster inside a
bloke if he doubts the whereabouts of his lady, he can
track her too on girlie nights out or shopping trips!
Perhaps the second one is a bit over the top, unless of
course he sees her firmly entrenched in Karen Millen
for an hour and considers the implication on Amex
next month!

So maybe the advent of the wonderful mobile phone
has caused problems and muchos 'nagging' distrust
and more than likely contributed to a break up more
than once.

Social Media

Another brilliant invention, one that has generated more 'nags' than are conceived at a stud top farm. Not only is it a forum for friends to comment on what your status say's and to fire a sarcastic little comment on the impulsive update keyed in seconds earlier, it is another link to the privacy question and thus a man's loyalty being questioned.

Where to start? Friend's, adding a friend that you have tracked down from school, college or work is part of the whole ethos of Facebook, keeping in touch and catching up on all of those memories. But that is the thing; the memories are history so why would a man accept a friend request from an old flame or a co-worker that is a possible suspected admirer? At his peril is the answer. Innocent or not befriending her is encouraging the flirting and deserves a bit of 'nagging' especially if he then likes a status or comments on a status, or if she likes or comments on an innocuous status of his own. It is just the same as putting a kiss on a text, if a comment has a "lol x" at the end, or "remember when we..." this can certainly cause some of the following little gems.

What does she mean by that?

"It's banter darling, she's just a Friend..."

Yeh right! That lame but accurate answer will really placate an inquisitive woman, good call! The fact that any man that encourages this banter shows enough reason to put a seed of doubt on the innocence, even for a split second.

The trouble is that today we use slang, poor grammar and poor punctuation in our everyday status updates, emails, text messages and so people read things they see in all of the above in a different way too, or how they want to read it. Most of us have no idea what the feck a Facebook friend actually means when they comment of a status, we just click the thumb icon and 'like' it to show we are potential stalkers maybe.

Why have you accepted her, you know I don't like her?

"Oh come on, it isn't important, jeez it was twenty years ago and lasted a week or two, plus she's married anyway, isn't that enough for you?"

Stand by your principals or back down? It isn't an easy choice but prepare to justify either decision, A lose and lost situation for sure; if a man un-friends the naughty girly then he is guilty of something, if he stays friends he is rubbing his woman's nose in it. He can't really win at all and there will always be a casualty, be it a long lost friend, his wife, or more likely himself. Once again hindsight rears its head to mock a man the advice was that he shouldn't have accepted her in the first place.

I see she made a comment on your status, think she fancies you!

"WTF, I said looking forward to a weekend away with you and she commented 'enjoy' that really translates to 'wish it was me' I give up!"

It must be all to do with a block in the brain that a woman has whereby reading a sentence is it then translated into a whole new collection of words. Another possible reason for reopening Bletchley Park to see if the Enigma Decoder can come up with a definitive guide for men and women and we can all finally understand what the other is saying or typing.

This appraisal is brought to you by stories from friends and family, not from personal experience, well perhaps a little, but thankfully Facebook entered my life after separating from my dear wife, and so the only personal experience I have is from mates telling me their stories of grief. Saying that think that in the early days of Friends Reunited I may have hooked up with a memory or two that required explanation, oh happy days!

The one thing that I can comment on is when I received a call only a few days after splitting from a lady and after a brief liaison. She might have been a little peeved in truth as the timing of the elbow action was poor on my part, Boxing Day to be exact, and despite the possibility that you might be thinking this was to do with the crap present she got me, it wasn't. Well part of it was but that is not important now. Anyway, for those au fait with the inner workings and display options of Facebook then you will know about the 'Relationship Status' tab. A user can choose from married, single, in a relationship, divorced, civil marriage, open relationship (a swinger probably) and even 'it's complicated' which I have always found a bit strange and a warning sign. My status was 'in a relationship' with ... and after the weight lifted off my shoulders that Boxing Day, soon after I decided to change it to single but only got half way before being distracted, by my daughter to play the Disney Game or similar. I deleted the said person's name but kept the 'in a relationship' bit. Can you see where this is going?

So, the home phone rings and off my daughter runs to get it, assuming it was a call from my ex-wife to say goodnight; oh no, it was the recently chucked woman and she asked my daughter to pass the phone over. My daughter obliged and also pulled a face to warm me of the tone she had used and I duly took the phone. Without a seconds hesitation I got an earful, something like this, "Who is she? You don't waste any time do you? How could you do this to me?"

Stunned, I managed to reply, "What the hell are you going on about?" and was then informed that she had seen my 'Relationship Status' as 'in a relationship' and obviously I was with someone new, less than 36 hours after showing her the door. After explaining that I had simply updated the obvious, that I wasn't with her anymore, she sheepishly apologised and bid her last farewell. A close call and a lesson or two learned, first, make sure that I NEVER 'add' another woman as a public relationship status and second, un-friend potential nutter's immediately. Think I made the right decision on that one.

Maybe the unwritten rule of social media is to keep partners off the friends list and to accept that the aforementioned bastion is intact to freely liaise without fear of reprisals. Perhaps this is why so many of my actual friends now don't have their partner as a Facebook friend? There is however the need to make sure that her friends or his friends is not a Facebook friend otherwise the information could get back of the comments and likes he or she make!

What a performance!

On that note it seems a good place to wrap up on social media and the dreaded mobile phone. But before we do, there is one more a little section on other interactions that can cause a problem, at work, and thus give a man reason to call 'nag alert.'

Work Liaisons

No not the office affair that you may have witnessed here and there, but the absolutely crazy things that lead to a comment or two that can make a man question his innocence, especially when he is totally innocent.

Cards, no not the poker hand, although a bit of bluffing is often used to get a man out of a hole that has been dug by a woman. Christmas, Birthday and Good Luck or 'Leaving' cards have caused a fracas on more than one occasion, and all down to what is inside the card itself.

Unless people at work decide to contribute the cost of sending cards to a charitable cause instead, then the annual exchange of cards is a potential pressure cooker for some couples. With a box of M&S or cheap cards purchased, the repetitive wrist strain from writing twenty or thirty cards to 'X and family' from 'Y and family' is nothing compared to the strain of receiving a card addressed to the recipient only and with no reference to his wife and kids, or even family. In addition if the card is signed off with 'lots of love' or 'love' or simply with XXX, no matter how nice and friendly this might appear it is just as bad as the text message received six months ago asking to come in late to work due to the toothache.

Why a kiss? or Only addressed to you, hmm?

"I don't bloody know, I didn't write the chuffing card!"
As if a man has any idea why a card, that he has brought home and put into the cardholder behind the door by the way, has NOT included his wife or HAS a friendly kiss on the bottom! If it were anything to worry about then perhaps he would have left it at work or burned the card in his wastepaper bin as a gesture to his chastity.

On the other side of equality, does a man inspect the cards for ones from her male colleagues and launch an investigation into the writing style, inference or luvvy duvvy sign off? No, because it MEANS .... ABSOLUTELY NAFF ALL!

No card from her this year, strange?
"Best ask her why, cause I really can't comment on who she has sent cards to, in a vague attempt to put your overactive mind at rest!"

Taking a roll call of who is working in the office and who bothered to send a card is a bit extreme to be honest, but it does happen, trust me! All of the examples in the book are hopefully isolated and down to a small number of women, or a man; that are incredibly insecure about their partner, but if the examples I have shared were totally normal, instead of being 'off the wall' then where would be the fun in highlighting them? None at all which is why there are more than a few and most of us have had experience with at least a little bit of the extreme examples.

Two plus two is four, but for a strange reason the answer is seven for certain people. By that what I am trying to get across is that a co-worker that sends daily texts, from holiday, but doesn't send a card at Christmas is obviously flirting, or is it that they did send a card and to avoid a slice of 'nag pie' the card was hidden or binned? Did the card have a kiss or a sultry comment that has nothing to do with festive greetings? Over analysis, and another example of how quantum physics can prove two plus two is seven!

Secret Santa has something to answer for as well, a bit of fun for 99.9% of us but when the mischief factor creeps in and the present chosen is a novelty item, such as a blow up doll kit or a dominatrix outfit, the gag can go sour when the unfortunate pressie is opened at home, or brought back home in the bag with the cards in.

Again, the inequality of a situation such as this never ceases to amaze me. If a woman brings home a Secret Santa from Ann Summers, batteries included, it means nothing. A man with a codpiece in a gift bag, however, is not auditioning for a place in the revival of the band Cameo, but can expect a genuine question to the origin of the ballsack; what's the word? "Up" or is it "nag"?

Who gave you that?

"I really don't know, that is why it is called 'Secret Santa' are you catching on with the concept?"

If the secret is actually that, a secret, then unless the mysterious elf owns up to the crime then it may be a secret forever. Does this help? Definitely not, but here's the thing it is a bit of fun and a festive frolic that makes no sense, that is what it is all about.

'Leaving Cards' complete the gift and bows part of this Chapter, and the solitary 'big card' will have a collection of good wishes for the future. Mixed in to the several 'good luck' comments it is possible that one or two signatories will add a personal comment like, "let me know if you need a wingman" or "thanks for coming." These are nice and demonstrate more than the clichés used on leaving cards, but what is the bet that the comment "going to miss our little chats" or "the place wont be the same without you and the fun and games we had" raise an eyebrow and further examination...

What fun, what games and how often did you have cosy little chats?

"Caught red handed, so sorry for being a sociable person at work and trying to enjoy the nine hours spent there Monday to Friday...perhaps I should have been a miserable shit instead!"

Working is upwards of 37.5 hours a week for full time people, with 47 or so weeks at work a year. That is 1,762.5 hours minimum; 105,750 minutes and if anyone is expected to never crack a joke, laugh at something or have a grown up chat about a film, holidays, weekend plans or anything else for that matter, then what a pathetic life it would be. Barmy as it might sound some couples do live in fear of their other half actually enjoying the day at work. Bonkers!

I kid you not, I know someone whose wife stated, "you were meant to be working, not enjoying yourself," said after his leaving do when she picked him up. As he said his final goodbyes on the pavement she had a quick look at his card and took umbrage to the comment from Sharon in data entry who jovially stated "gonna miss your gags, and your smile," and from the back seat, I sat in silence, flabbergasted at the onslaught. Thanks for the short lift though!

Leading on from the point made about general chit chat at work there is the subject of borrowing things from fellow workers. A copy of the latest DVD blockbuster movie, not that I am condoning any breach of the copyright conditions, a copy of Fifty Shades, no, not of Nagging, the other ones. The same goes for bringing an adult movie home, not that I ever have, but some old workmates have come unstuck after sharing the unofficial company library of porn. Not a good move if their better half is a regular churchgoer!

Here I go again, implying that the lewd side of life is commonplace amongst the male of the species. Lap dancing clubs, porn, chatting women up, secrets ... this is NOT what it is like being a man but plenty of women think that this is what men are ALL are like and get up to away from their gaze. Twaddle, but if a bloke or one of his mates does the 'Carry On Film' routine and throws an innuendo it sets the cogs spinning and that inevitable doubt on how they behave when they are out. This then justifies the spot check on a fellas phone or a quick check on the phone finder App.

We haven't even looked at email accounts or checking the browsing history on the home PC. That would cover another few pages of observations, however I really cannot imagine how intrusive this is or the blushing faces if a woman finds a message from bird on a dating site, saying 'he' has a new wink or a new message from a 'her' or worse a conversation from a woman that is consoling a partner who is having a moan about his 'nagging' wife. Hacking a partners email account is bad enough but staying logged on is asking for trouble if there is something to hide, what a complete jerk! It goes to show that if anyone looks hard enough they will find evidence that points to some indiscretion if the evidence could be deciphered as an indiscretion at all.

Browsing history is another issue completely. If the websites visited are open to review and include one or two adult themed portals, then it is always going to raise an eyebrow if it pops up on the warning list for the internet security. Naughty naughty!

Why is it as dramatic as I make out? Easy answer, men let themselves down throughout a relationship; they drop in a comment, opinion or worse fall foul to an urge and bang!...Their card is marked. This ongoing journey through life and relationships then suffer for the one day out of ten years that they messed up. That is what women remember and bring up, just to put a man in his place or to remind him that a certain heffalump never forgets!

The third screen aside, the journey through the 'Life of Pie' reaches the stagnant time, when couples accept to live together and chip away at each other on a regular basis, thus accepting the status quo, or they rebel and from controversy, confrontation starts. The next Chapter looks at the time when 'nagging turns to war' and defense mechanisms kick in, attack by words can get out of control and even after splitting, the 'nagging' continues.

6
Mid Life Crisis

Let the Fun Begin

Fun for some, but not for all, when that age bracket, between thirty and fifty, arrives a little demon pops up on your shoulder and starts whispering things in your ear... "Don't take that, give her some back," or "Enough already, just ignore it.... for now!"

Men often become 'nag blind' and don't even see a sharp comment anymore, which is like red rag to our female bull; there is no such thing I hear you say, and you would be right, but how insulting to my female readers to say "red rag to a cow!" Whatever the phrase used here is it doesn't alter the fact that in ignoring the suggestions made by a woman it flaming well annoys them. What to do? Intensify the 'nagging' to beat a man into submission or find multiple things to say in the hope that the crescendo of comments inspires a positive reaction and he picks up a paint-brush or plugs in the vacuum cleaner.

And so, after a few years of harmonious life the 'game of slice' takes on new meaning and 'nagging' basically turns into arguing over the smallest of things for millions of couples. The little demons sitting on both shoulders have a field day encouraging snappy retorts that earn points in the ongoing game and thus counteract points lost to a volley of abuse and the occasional drop shot to the baseline.

The decision is whether to play the game or take the huff and pick up the toys and walk away. If it were only as simple as a game of Monopoly!

If either a man or woman decide to keep playing the game then like millions of couples they will bat the ball back and forth for years, one winning a game here and the other the next, and so on. Some play the game as a soft exchange of shots while others engage in full-blown forehand and backhand shots, hit as hard as possible. We see it every day in public when an older couple obviously cant stand each other and she announces to everyone in ear shot what a waste of space he is, just the same way as Nora Batty used to in 'Last of the Summer Wine', hated that programme but when growing up with one TV in the house and then three channels, BBC1 BBC2 and ATV, you didn't get much of a choice. Saying that seeing my dad cringe and feel for the old bloke taking the verbal beating was funny, and a formative moment for me, "that will not be happening to me!" Ahh hindsight, it makes no difference for some things. No idea what the little man that rolled his 'R's" was called, but pretty sure he made a few quid voicing the Hovis advert on the side, fair play to him!

Enough of Compo and crew, save the fact that this limited visual choice on the television demonstrated what COULD be said to a man, and indeed so true to life, a 'Life of Pie.'

A man who decided that a great excuse for his antics was to give it a medically sounding condition probably conceived the phrase 'Mid Life Crisis'. Perfect now there was a real excuse out of his control and he was off the hook. No way Pedro, if that was his name, it's not that easy chap! Mid Life Crisis is NOT an excuse for spending the family savings on a flash motorcar, to yearn for youth again, or engage in very naughty shenanigans with a 20 year old, just for the sake of it.

The same goes for a woman who has a crisis too and decides that the grass is greener or because he said 'this or that' to her which is a free pass to find a 20 or 30 year old playmate. Whatever the cardinal sin that might have happened the funny thing is that men and women look for other excuses to defend the situation, should they be questioned?

When Nagging Turns to War

Inevitably 'nagging' turns sour in a lot of cases, which is why we have a generation chucking the towel in at the moment when the 'nagging' turns into those arguments no doubt. Indeed I was going to call the book 'Fifty Shades More – When Nagging Turns to War' but decided that this was probably a bit negative and another catharsis offering that would lose the intended funny side of the communication pie chart of life. Too many grey areas to consider and certainly less humorous!

Including examples of arguments is therefore not going to be funny, in fact probably the opposite, especially if you have been on the receiving side of them, but here's the thing, there are clichés used in any breakdown of a relationship that are ridiculously funny and deserve a mention.

Well if you don't care then I don't either
"Fine by me, you finally got the hint"
Tit for tat, a cry for help or whatever it actually translates to "I do care you git" and "I do too, but I am sure as hell not going to admit it!"

Drop the onslaught and revert to talking as grown

ups is a better solution, but do we act as grown ups when faced with this preliminary statement to the real argument, do we bugger!

This is your last chance!

"What again? Cheers, I'm sure I will muck it up again but I suppose it's a lifeline for now!"

How many last chances does anyone get? As many as allowed is the simple answer and this little ultimatum is like red rag to a bull, using the correct gender attachment this time.

Other veiled threats can emanate from the mouth of a woman, things that she will do to make you really suffer, such as the next one.

*If you let me down one more time I will ....
(either)…a) Take you for everything, b) Kick you out, or perhaps c) Shag all your mates!*

There is no witty response to either of these optional threats except following the retaliatory suggested courses of action, to either a) spend your money just in case, b) change the locks first while she is out, or c) tell your first mates that she has chlamydia and a reaction to rubber so condoms can't be used. What the heck are any of these forewarned outcomes about anyway, especially the third one? Is the third one a figment of my overactive imagination, actually no it isn't and I couldn't believe it when I heard it; whether it is a personal experience or not I will let you decide. Either way you have got to be kidding me, how ridiculous would it be to get back at a man by bedding his mates, and more importantly after the sharing of knowledge that men and women partake in on lads and girlie nights out, even if she is a hot blond with

32EE's. Seriously though there are plenty of shallow blokes out there that would take up on an offer to sleep with a friends ex-wife while she is still with their friend, so after a break up why would it be different? The only saving grace is that they may consider the risk after seeing what misery she bestowed on the friend and the very real potential of her turning into that bird on the Exorcist?

Warning phrases aside, these are exchanges that are usually in the early stages and before the real falling out that leads to one or other making a decision to go.

If the constant 'nagging' and arguments go on for months, if not years, then deciding to throw it all way is a distinct possibility. Attempting to save it could be an option and then counseling is suggested, common ground to talk through the issues with a suitably trained volunteer. What a great forum, both sit there with a stranger and both plead their case for what they honestly believe, he is a useless arse and she is a vindictive cow. Adopting the philosophy that it is 'better out than in' the warring couple hope that the mediator takes sides and backs either up in the justified comments. The mediator, whether a he or a she, will probably sit and listen and use that calm voice to suggest they dig deeper into the issue, job done and £30 for the sounding block, cheers!

Wouldn't it be great if a mediator or counselor actually gave an opinion, just for fun to stir it up a bit more, for example, "He has a point, tracking his phone is a bit over the top, you insecure bint!" or "Well, what do you expect you clart! Coming home over eight hours after popping out for a quick half, returning bladdered and wearing different clothes?" But alas this honesty is probably a contradiction to the advertised service, from the charity funded help centres, to listen for free but pay for the time anyway!

It's Over

What is it about breaking up, whether as a sixteen year old or a grown up, that turns a person into a character from a movie and the apparent need to use a cliché when a heartfelt bit of honesty would be received far better? Maybe it is the hope that keeping someone in limbo is nicer and softens the blow, when the blow is inevitable.

I am certainly not belittling the emotional impact of a break up at all, ooh serious again, but after all if the 'nagging' has gone too far or the recipient is numb then it will probably get messy from here in. So why leave things in limbo, and more importantly why come out with garbage like these comments?

I need some space!

"Space dust? Space 1999? Or is it a code for drugs that I don't know about?

What is 'space' and why is 'space' said with those two fingers raised at shoulder height, like two 'naked' yet unoffensive Fingerbobs or the two little birds, Peter and Paul from the nursery rhyme? Probably to add weight to the word and symbolise the importance of 'space' as a word using gesticulation and air painted explanation marks.

It is, however, a golden ticket opportunity but some men don't see it as that because they want to fix things, explain or convince instead, to make it all better.

A perfect opportunity to let a woman get her head together and while doing so they can escape the daily 'nagging' for a while and let everything cool down for a rational conversation, later after a bit of apart time.

On the other hand having some 'space' can simply give a woman time to prepare the case for the prosecution, ably assisted by the female only back room team that provide support and opinion. Or change the locks, move a work colleague in to share the rent and under that 'innocent tenant' disguise, maybe to share the marital bed on cold nights too. Not much 'space' found there then, hope the snoring doesn't keep you awake!

Not always the case but how often does 'space' get filled rather quickly?

It's not you it's me
"That makes a change it's normally me"

The prelude to the next comment that a decision is made and that it is over and no matter what further explanation will follow for the moment, at least, the towel has been thrown in and to avoid a fight it is easier to take the easy option to take the blame and bug out.

Lines borrowed from the script of a movie, full of melancholy, and with very little that anyone can do to respond other than with a sarcastic retort and just having a bit of fun for the sake of it! Replying with, "yes you are probably right and I really agree with you actually, the constant criticism, carping and shouting is wholly inappropriate; but thanks for admitting it!" Yes, a cheap shot and very unlikely that a bloke would actually say it, but you can bet your life he is thinking it as relief and sadness mull over him. Of course if he did issue a wounded reply then he could certainly expect a juicy reply in return.

Men use this phrase too and then blame themselves for not being able to 'commit' which is a word like 'space' WTF does commit mean, answers on a postcard please or via the Twitter page! Seriously 'commit' is what we all do, or at least should do and so bugging out due to a lack of commitment is ludicrous. It must be a fear of something, or a phobia maybe? Gynophobia, that will be it but what is the bet that it is not Genophobia, and any fear of sex will dissapear as soon as a man can together with a new woman, until they get bored and state "It's not you, it's me and I can't commit....you deserve better!" Blinder!

Get out of my house!

"Your house, that's a good one, in case you haven't noticed it is our house and I got the land registry deeds to prove it luvvy!"

OK so things aren't going that well but what is the assumption that a man is the one to leave all about? Who knows but one thing is for sure a woman honestly believes that when a marriage or relationship breaks up that the house is hers, no matter what, and this the only gallant thing left is for the man to pack his bags and go. There is only one word for it, 'austere' and even more ridiculous if they are separating at her instigation. Is this a sign of things to come?

The cliché is occasionally replaced with the guilt trip comment to encourage a man to leave so as to give her some 'space' (Eureka, now that word 'space' has meaning!) and instead of demanding he leaves the home, she might encourage him to go in a nice way with a hint that it is best for everyone, for a short time of course. Once out the locks can be changed and even a key given to that young bloke at work soon after, only as a back up if she is locked out of course!

Making the decision is a false sense of security for men and women and both probably think that the worst of the arguing is over but for many 'nagging' and retaliation takes on a whole new meaning.

Post Relationship Nagging

If all fails and breaking up is inevitable, then the relief from 'nagging' that people say they get is short lived. Yes perhaps the 'nagging' under the same roof stops but it is replaced by equally weighted 'nagging' from separate houses. I could go on for pages and pages on the subject of a 'new game' surrounding the rights and wrongs of divorce and the involvement of solicitors that position a sparring couple perfectly to fight the good or bad fight, but I will refrain from this opinion for obvious legal reasons and leave the interpretation of right and wrong to others to write about. That being said, the one big thing that continues to annoy men and women is the share of the booty.

Financial disclosure is part of the divorce process and the wonderful Form E is required to show everyone how much a man or a woman has stashed away so that, in the majority of cases the woman can go for the maximum due to her. So, from a decision to cash the chips in a man can find that his chips are worth less than face value, plus he has the 'ability' to earn more so doesn't need as much of the equity! Oh yes, that is a fine counter argument to the patriarchist's, or perhaps it helps their cause, yes that will be it!

Completing these lovely multi-page documents means copying bank statements and filling in owned items over a certain value. This tedious task is a load of baloney anyway as it is only a snapshot and if either party is cute they can fill it in before payday when the overdraft is maxed out...genius! The funny part of it is the definition and inclusion of things and so for those that have never had the pleasure of filling out a Form E, here is the quick alternative user guide for men and women.

- *Vehicles - Men must include their car and any outstanding loan against it. Women can include their car, however any loan is still down to him!*
- *Jewelery - Men must include family air looms such as valuable watches or similar. Women don't need to include the engagement ring, wedding ring or grannies diamond encrusted chunk of gold. Because they are her costume jewelery!*
- *Savings - any joint accounts are theirs and should be placed in escrow, but any savings in her name can be spent now, any in his name can't.*
- *Valuations - any other family air looms passed down from his mother should be treated as theirs and valued at three times their maximum estimated auction price. Any from her mother will be valued at negligible auction estimate or a paltry reserve value…just saying!*

Now, the exchange of Form E's can also raise a few questions when an estranged partner digests the bank statements in detail and the credits and debits for the last few months. The intention is to steer the negotiation between both parties, however more often causes more problems than it is worth and doubt creeps in.

You must have money hidden away!

"Hang on I will check under the mattress, nope it is all there on the signed document; wish I did but savings never really built up my side with overindulgence in the buying department"

Hindsight is a wonderful thing and stashing a couple of million away in premium bonds is very attractive after the event. It is only a shame that men don't have the ability to gaze into the future the same way as women can isn't it!

Is this down to years of bickering over who pays for what and then when the man pays on his card he obviously has money she didn't know about? I suppose that this does make sense and justifies the impression that he has a little pot of gold, because he always seemed to find the money to finance their extravagant life style. Nope the Form E clearly states the appalling debt built up on credit cards and loans...just to keep the peace or with the knowledge that the equity in the house was always going to provide access to funds. Foolish now! The house gone, err ..yer screwed chap!

I see you had a lovely Valentines Meal – hope she was worth it!

"Huh? Oh, the debit card entry that hit my account on 14th February that means I went out on a date. Err actually no it may have hit my account that day but it was a bite to eat with X, male, six feet and a lifelong friend not a fudge packer buddy!"

Apart from the fact that it is absolutely none of an estranged wife's business if a man wants to go out and especially if she was shacked up with a certain wonder-bollocks and probably got more than a card on that Valentine's Day to boot.

It is uncomplicated; they were 'on a break' exactly the same as Ross and Rachael on 'Friends.' By the way we all know how well that went for Ross in the end!

Using a lovely legal phrase, 'notwithstanding', this decision to refrain from comment about the ruthless yet wonderful and lovely divorce lawyers in the World, there are some more ridiculous comments that are clearly said by a woman and a man under advisement from their brief. I may be a little harsh here too as I am sure that it is not just lawyers that suggest these little comments, there are friends and family that also suggest standing firm and slicing at a soon to be ex-husband, the jugular is a favourite big vein to slice at. Okay not a vein, an artery but I am playing word association with another blue vein.

Not all women are this ruthless, thankfully but for every amicable split there is definitely a story from hell out there.

The saddest part is the bickering over a few quid, the funniest part is that for the first time in many a year they both become as tight as a ducks ringpiece.

You owe me!

"What for? Oh my mistake for you taking the house and now the clear financial responsibility for me to pay your bills too, silly me!"

How on earth is this assumption made? It is more than likely down to the festering animosity fueled by a bunch of her friends that quietly demand that she gets what is due to her. Fair enough but if the peer group contains a control freak that is most definitely a misanthropist, a recent divorcee that is still reeling from the break up, another two that are getting over their hubbies affairs, it is likely that the moral support is nothing less than tantamount to loading the bullets and passing the gun over for the head shot!

I've got a bill for you

"What's that? Oh, something that you have agreed to and assumed that it is down to me to fork out for – stupid me and I thought that is what maintenance was for?"

Extras, all extras and defined by the historic fact that the man always paid for the previous bills out of his account. Another reason to why the Form E clearly shows 'naffallpence' in savings accounts.

There are most likely hundreds of niggling phrases that surround the negotiation that takes place after a relationship ends, all of which could fill a book with the alternative answers and replies that a man would like to say, if he had the confidence to do so.

The expectation of sharing liability and therefore the need to state the demand in a new forceful way, without fear of upsetting a partner, isn't reserved to monetary issues alone; looking after the kids is another area of debate.

After years of doing the family bit there is a new freedom for the husband and wife, to enter the cattle market in search of new stock. This in turn means the sharing of weekend child minding duties while also sharing the free nights to razz it up. Men go on a 'nag free' outing safe in the knowledge that they can come home when they like and without repercussion the following morning. They can get bladdered and attempt to pull a young heifer only to end up with a cow that has seen better days, if indeed she can see with her one eye!

Women can get into a pickle too in the cattle market that is the 'local club'; young bulls might be attracted by little red dresses and at the risk of being labelled a cougar or MILF the chance to have some fun with a younger man is too good an opportunity to pass up. This is bad news for the men who are of the same age, but clearly they are far too old and past it for a newly liberated woman! For the moment at least, however maybe after a few flings the older and wiser man will perhaps appeal again, them being on a similar wavelength and at least able to recognise what a Rubik's Cube was all about, not think that it is merely an image that record companies use on 80s compilation CD's.

Arranging a night out can be at the last minute when either a bunch of girls take the initiative and arrange to hit the town and so a man can get a text or a phone call late in the week asking, or even telling him that he is on dad duty. Forget his own plans it is his obligation to accept the request and let her do her thing! After all she might find another bloke to start on so it could be a result to divert 'nagging' away. Win-win!

So, in the evolutional journey we are on a woman can certainly achieve new found heights in her ability to 'nag' and whether it is 'nagging' at an estranged husband or at a new fella, her art can be refined with the confidence only gained by experience.

A man may experience an enforced freedom and as he exchanges his abode from the one he has helped to craft over many years of toil for a one bedroom flat with paper walls and regular interruptions from a herd of elephants walking upstairs and wild boar snoring loudly next door, he may ponder what it would have been like to still be at the marital home and subject to 'Silver Surfer Nagging'. Which by mere coincidence is the next Chapter.

7
Silver Surf Nagging

Right then, shall we make the assumption that not every relationship ends with separation and divorce? I think we should because even though roughly 40-45% or marriages end in divorce, according to the Office for National Statistics, that leaves over half that survive and thus provide us with plenty of observation of married couples that become 'Silver Surfer Naggers'.

This therefore is the next part of the journey through a 'life of nagging' and allows us to look deeper at the funny things that people say to each other after reaching the half-century and beyond.

Many couples get through the trials and tribulations of married life and succeed where many others fail, staying together, building a nest egg for retirement and by agreeing to disagree on plenty of issues while maintaining some balance in the relationship. This balance might be tipped in favour of the woman having her say, or in favour of the bloke who has carved out a life with work, down time with his buddies and maybe some self-flagellation as penance for his selfish attitude!

Having a hobby or two, taking part in sport and also enjoying quality time together is one way that older couples manage to carry on with a loving relationship and therefore graduate to the 'silver surfer nagging' phase. Somewhere between the mid life crisis and another change that takes place in a woman's life things can get heated and can certainly contribute to some off the wall 'nagging' which she doesn't even realise she is issuing. The change I refer to is 'the change' or to use the proper word 'the menopause'. Forget the hormone imbalance that occurs every 28 days or so for the majority of her life; when the cycle stops, or slows down, the levels of oestrogen fall and the effect on memory is something a man should watch out for. A woman will forget some things thankfully, be a bit foggy on others and thus partial memory will mean she might remember the bad things. The answer is Premarin or other hormone replacement therapies and when the balance is restored a man can be grateful that she will remember everything again most likely. Utter joy!

The other effects of the menopause, such as the dreaded migraines, increased stress and rapid mood changes are all part and parcel of the 'Life of Pie' and some of the most intense 'nagging' comments can cut a man to the bone without a woman actually meaning it for a change. One other symptom, the flushes and night sweats should not however be mistaken for a wet dream by any man; they are not a subconscious invitation to 'hop on board' unless invited to do so!

How Many Times?

In public many couples are so obviously still in the relationship because it is the easy option, they don't even like each other! They are used to each other and think they know each other, yes but they bicker and thus raise a smile for onlookers to witness with lovely comments like these...

No, No, No the wholemeal - listen next time!

Dispatched to get a loaf from the bread aisle, how often do men receive a carping comment when they come back to the trolley with the wrong loaf or bag of flour, poor sods!

Will you hurry up, I haven't got all day

Picture the woman walking ahead while the love of her life is trailing behind, struggling to keep up as they engage on another shopping mission to buy some chops from the butcher and a nice piece of fish from the fishmongers. The classic stereotype is a largish woman and a frail looking little man that looks like he used to be six feet tall but has been 'nagged' so much that he is now five feet seven!

Behind closed doors the usual fault finding clichés are mixed with periods of harmony and apart from the others that we have already looked at, let's have a final look at the 'standard' ones that men hear every day somewhere in the world, and again some of the quick replies that we would love to say to win a point back!

You don't fancy me anymore!

"Well I would if I thought you actually liked me at all, bit difficult when all I seem to do is wind you up!"

How on earth can either a man or woman be attracted to the other if constant bickering takes place?

'Chastising someone leads to chastity.'

You don't understand

"How the hell can I, I'm a bloke and will never, never understand how a woman thinks!"

Men try to understand but with all the curve balls that

they get it 'mushes their brains' and logic disappears, hence there is no way that they will ever truly understand what a woman means. After all as I said right at the end of the first book, 'what man utters, woman chooses not to hear' and so why is it any different when the roles are reversed?

You are always doing ...
"Well excuse me for having a life!"

Yes, some men only do their own stuff and neglect their spouse. Whether it is football in their twenties, replaced by cricket in their thirties and then golf until their seventies or fishing all the way through life it means hours away from home and a clear indication that they would rather be elsewhere. In reality these hobbies are what keeps a man sane and deep down they would like to see their woman do the same, as long as it isn't golf too! Only kidding, but if a woman does take up golf then the realisation that a round takes under four hours will then put into question the years of her man being at the golf club for six hours every Saturday. Once the obligatory travel time has been factored in the sudden realisation is that for years he has been sitting in the male lounge sipping a pint and discussing what other men's wives have been 'nagging' about during the previous week, comparing notes, instead of rushing home to take her shopping or trim the lawn!

Although it is wonderful to see a couple in their 80's walking hand in hand, or at least sharing a Zimmer frame, this is an all too rare site; more often it is the vacant look as they shuffle around the shops and in the queue for the bus. Silence over a cup of tea at House of Fraser is a weekly treat and if you happen to be there with your own mother then you spot the silent couple. Are they all 'talked out' after 50 years of baking and consuming 'nag pie' or is the level of conversation just so repetitive they already know the answers to the regular questions? Questions like

Have you taken your Wulfren?
"Yes dear"

Ahh medication and the need for two pill boxes with seven compartments labelled with the following idiot proof letters, M, T, W, T, F, S and S. Indeed Monday morning's job, written on the calendar as a reminder, is to fill each pill box with a variety of prescription drugs so that they don't forget. One box will have a dob of nail varnish to differentiate it from her hormone replacement drugs as god forbid he takes one or two Premarin by mistake! The calendar will have family birthdays along with when the OJ (orange juice) was opened to avoid food poisoning by going over the strict four-day 'use within' warning.

Have you checked the oil in the car?
"Yes dear"

Nothing left to do for retirees than take the pills and make sure the car is checked weekly for the correct oil level and tyre pressure. Oh my life there is something to look forward to, especially the regular check that the oil check has been done.

Do you want fish for your tea?
"Yes dear"

This is another example of the 'routine' that enters pensioners lives in the salad years and the level of communication, what happened to spontaneity and fun? It's now merely a conversation stopper over a nice hot cuppa and an Eccles cake. Followed by more silence for a minute or two before the forced attempt to talk in sentences of more than two words. Some old age pensioners have taken to reading a magazine during these regular outings to the store restaurant or local garden centre café. She, digesting the contents of Woman's Own and he, hiding a copy of FHM inside Advanced Carp Fishing!

How was your cake?

"Nice dear"

Not a descriptive response by any means, of course it could be down to then fact that a purchased piece of carrot cake is nice whereas if he goes into detail on how moist and tasty it is he might run the risk of offending her baking skills and years of experience has taught him to be nondescript!

If they opt for an item off the menu then she might choose for him and he will get what he gets! "Ooh I do love a bit of salmon, let's have two of those" never mind if he wants the quiche, the choice is made.

Good Old Mother!

Perhaps the lack of response from husbands is the reason why mothers turn their attention to sons to keep their hand in 'nagging' after their now lifelong practice and immense talent for 'nagging.'

The lack of spontaneity with everything else in a widowed mothers life is down to the need to have a routine, be that a weekly 'big shop' or the need to know what a son is doing daily. If he 'usually' goes to London on a Tuesday but works from home on a Wednesday then he will be 'available' to take a call on Wednesday. If he swaps his week around then he is subject to phone 'nagging' if he isn't in. She needs a job doing and she wants it done NOW, not later. How dare he change his week without telling her! It is almost like he has altered his routine to annoy her on purpose or to have an excuse for not being able to change a light bulb until later in the week when he is available and will not jeopordise his work and run the risk of getting a P45, that's a pink slip in the US!

You might have told me it was Jan and Jim's 50ᵗʰ Anniversary!

"How the hell was I supposed to know, I wasn't at the bloody wedding was I?"

Close family birthdays, parties, milestones in other peoples lives, anniversaries from distant relatives or when the sewing bee is due to meet are not things that a son adds to his iCal on his Mac. They are things that he has no input or even interest in unless it effects his social obligations. They are things that mothers usually write on the kitchen calendar, along with the OJ opened dates and doctors appointments.

Now if a mother misses someone's Golden Wedding Anniversary, for a relative, or even a couple from the church, why is it her son's fault when she realises the error? Where does the blame factor actually equate? Exactly, it doesn't, but the disturbing fact is that mothers actually believe that it is their children's obligation to remind their parents of up and coming events and important dates. If they don't then they can expect, "well you didn't remind me" which is also bizarre because mothers still manage to remind sons to send a card to someone else on the calendar! Let's not revisit the instructions to send cards to people, these were covered in the first book quite clearly.

Where have you been, I have been calling for days!

"Sorry, I actually don't dial 1471 just in case you didn't leave a message, because that kinda contradicts what an answer machine is for!"

I am sure that mothers don't leave a message so that they can catch a son out for not calling for a few days. When they ask "where you have been?" this not only reinforces their need to know, even if they don't need to know, but is also an opportunity to offer an opinion about what it is that the son has been doing. In fact they probably log the attempted call on the calendar next to the dates and the note for 'OJO' (orange juice opened).

Can you take me to the ...

"Have I got a 'private hire' license on my bumper? Maybe not but that doesn't matter does it, you need to go half a mile and thus it makes sense for me to drive five miles to pick you up and drive five back!"

Son-Cabs is actually a pretty good idea for a business concept, pick up mothers and charge a fiver for a trip charged direct the actual son's debit card. Just think of the time saved for both. Quick service collection and assistance with the seat belt all included in the nominal fiver charge. The passenger could receive a complimentary voucher that they can instantly exchange for 'one nag' for either driving too fast or for saying the 'f' word at the old codger in front! Regular users could build up loyalty points to exchange for a half an hour wait outside the hospital, dentist or incontinence clinic.

Over time additional services could be offered for nominal cost such as the weekly shop to include pick up and drop off, complimentary trolley push and a flask of tea for sustenance halfway through the two-hour aisle experience. No added extras would be charged for waiting behind the Renault Clio driven by the lady pensioner who likes to wait for a space at the front of the supermarket car park, causing grid-lock behind, or the Austin Allegro driven by a bloke in a flat cap that takes nine or ten goes to reverse out of the space.

Indeed a 'no surcharge guarantee' for time delays or even 'danger money' for the driver is another plus point. Danger and delay due to the lunatic pensioner that reverses out without looking before driving the wrong way around the car park. There is a superb marketing opportunity here though, as the Son-Cab driver could have a voucher or flyer that he thrusts onto the windscreen as the old boy drives past and clips his wing mirror, a maneuverer that is as scary as hell and carried out with a shake of the head as if to imply he is in the right. It is always a good look, flat cap, a look of utter disgust on his face as he strug-gles to look over the square steering wheel!

To provide a final bit of service excellence Son-Cabs could offer a door-to-door service, thus would go and get the car from the other end of the car park and then drive to the supermarket entrance to block the thoroughfare by loading the big shop into the boot. Wrong as it might be to cause a lovely traffic jam, the precedent is clearly set by elderly couples that do it anyway, especially the bloke in the Austin Allegro.

I think this has some legs, might write into the Dragon's Den team!

Perhaps it is an age thing but lots of older people are into religion in a big way. The Church, Synagogue, Mosque or Temple is not only a place to worship but they are also a place to fund raise and bake a cake or ten to sell to the local community. By definition baking for the church fair requires raw materials, flour, sultanas, lemons and believe it or not whisky for the flavouring. It is therefore obligatory that if a son owns a bottle of highland malt then it should be donated for a good cause as part of the fundraising.

Getting the heavy stuff is also a task he should be willing to do, price limits are set after to buy the flour at Asda then drive to Tesco to get the fruit because Tesco flour is 1p cheaper than Asda and visa versa. The reason that she knows this isn't down to surfing the Internet on price comparison sites, far from it, it is purely hearsay from Dot who told her about the offer after sending her husband out on the weekly supermarket crawl, driving five miles in one direction to save a few pence. The petrol cost is irrelevant here and while Dot's husband actually enjoys bargain hunting and probably spends more, after the fuel cost is then factored in, at least he is doing something proactive and building up brownie points. A very clever man in my opinion!

In addition to the supermarket dash attending the event and contributing is expected. Bringing the family to have a cuppa and a slice of cake, presented on blue crockery from the Second World War is the start. Paying 20p for a second hand book, such as the 1982 Shoot Annual and a few 10p tries on the tombola to win a very sought after Bromley Soap Set. The last bit of change in the pocket might go on a crocheted teapot cover for the teapot you don't own, £2.55 lighter and more stuff for the everything drawer, bliss.

Before anyone thinks is another opportunity for Son-Cabs to take over the role and transport the cakes to the cold church hall and mingle with the church members, it probably isn't. Why? Because an unknown taxi driver cannot engage in conversation about the days when they were dragged kicking and screaming to church every week and or, as mentioned in the first book, get mistaken for their elder brother.

Any son that submits to the request to help their mother at the church fair also runs the risk of letting her down if the subject matter turns to belief and possible request to join the church by the vicar to boost falling numbers. Dangerous ground if the son is, like many of his generation, a bit of a non-believer. Try to remember that Atheism never goes down well at the church fair!

The rules of the game are therefore quite simple, respect a the views of a parent with regards to religion and debate in private not in front of the vicar, rabbi, imam, pujari or any pious person!

These, shall we say, differing opinions on the very sensitive subject of religion can lead to some 'nagging' comments on the way home.

How dare you question God!

"Because I am a grown up and watch the Discovery Channel, shall we debate evolution now?"

Probably not the best response, but entering into the science versus church debate is certainly more fun than discussing hip replacement's and the £376.57 raised at the church fair. Here's the thing, believing or not believing in scripture is a choice however much the same as every opinion that a mother has, she is unlikely to change and so it is probably best to let her vent her frustration that you entered into an theology debate with the vicar on the seven days to craft the earth compared to the millions of years of happenchance that saw man evolve from a furry ape. Just saying!

The thing to remember here is that religion is as much a 'nagging' platform as the words that come out of a womans mouth. Think about it. Preachers, that have a divine opinion, have used criticism against people that do anything wrong, with the weight of a god behind them to demand penance for centuries. Standing in pulpits they use "thou must" phrases to ensure sinners are penitent. It is just the same as 'nagging'.

You have turned that child into an atheist!

"That child? Oh your granddaughter who happens to have an opinion of her own...hmmm maybe it was the fact that she recognised very early that Santa was a hoax, the Easter Bunny was a bit of a lie and that her own science class discussed Darwin last term!"

On the other hand being browbeaten as a child at the various Sunday school's to the validity of the stories in the old and new testaments didn't convince a generation that it was the place to go on a Sunday for everyone, some swapped it for a lie in! Sitting back and watching the debate between a daughter and grandmother is however hilarious! I know I am going to hell for this outrageous opinion as well as for being that misogynist that women think I am. Or is there a hell at all? Sorry I am off again, but only because that naughty gene I inherited from an ancestor thinks it is funny to tweak a nerve here and there. No doubt mother, various other aunties and cousins will probably read this and shake their heads in disgust. What can I say; the apple fell far from the tree! Oh, and so did my brothers apple too!

8
On The Other Hand

Now on to the Chapter that offers counter opinion to the so-called misogynistic views that many women will read from the previous seven chapters. Well maybe not counter opinion, more of a précis of the various ages of a man and some insight into the trials and tribulations men have to go through to find their way in life.

In some ways the most difficult chapter to write, actually no it wasn't, because part of any man's life is to, at some point, stop and consider if and when he has been a complete dickhead and caused problems for himself. This self-flagellation is part of his realisation and unfortunately it comes far too late in life to make any difference.

This isn't an apology or acceptance of errors for the male species, rather a look at the journey through life for men, the things men say and how they contribute to the communication breakdown.

Shall we start with infants and progress to teen-agers, adolescent's and cocky twenty year olds before finally looking at mature gentlemen and their funny ways. This coincides with a time in their own exis-tence when they often have no energy left to conjure up a dubious excuse? I think we should.

This Chapter fits in nicely with a suggestion that I

write a book called 'Fifty Shades of Bragging' with the main subject matter based on how some men, if not the majority, impose their opinions on others in a cocky manner. Opinions and excuses perpetuated with a hint of bullshit! In fact maybe it is a 'Life of Bragging'!

Out of the Mouths of Babes

No, I am not referring to the biblical reference in the Old and New Testaments, and most certainly not to any wisdom that a small child has, especially a small boy.

If I were then I would also include the numerous references to 'nagging' that are contained in the bible, some say upwards of 40! Or, that I would quote a verse or two such as "a continual dripping on a rainy day and a quarrelsome wife are alike" Proverbs 27:15; because they were all written and approved by men as the debate over what books and verses should be included in the approved bible's have been over the centuries, ever since the First Council of Nicaea in AD 325.

Yes some things clearly stuck in my mind from those years of lost Sunday mornings at 'Sunday School', probably the only bit of preaching that I have taken with me through life! Perhaps it was my father that pointed out the verses?

No, the reference to what comes out of a small males child's mouth is often copying what they hear from their father, but they also learn to say other comments that are nothing less than little fibs.

Little boys can be horrid, demanding selfish and compulsive liars in truth and whether it is part of the learning curve to find a place in the pecking order of whatever.

From an early age the potential to get away with

an outburst and thus take the 'overinflated opinions' through life become second nature.

Small boys plead innocence when accused of breaking something or other, and blame sisters or even the wind to avoid the wrath of parents. How many times will a parent hear "I didn't do it!" when the child most definitely has 'done it'!

As far as bragging goes we have all overheard a boy tell other kids that "I went there" or "I have one too" when they haven't been at all or don't have a particular item. It is the start of a slippery slope for boys that will eventually grow into adults, who also need to save face with their peers and so they bullshit to keep up with what their friends have done or where they have been. But more of these fabricated lies later in the Chapter.

Maybe the reason why boys become smaller clones or versions of their fathers is the same as why girls become smaller versions of their mothers. Here's where we get into the psychobabble and how grown up's nurture their offspring, thus teaching them how to act and react with people.

A domineering father who is a control freak will teach their son to be the same, to be strong and not to let a woman have their say. Draconian in todays society but nevertheless probably what his opinioniated father's father taught him.

For millennia men have dominated society and changing to a more 'balanced and equitable arrangement' is only a hundred or so years old itself. Indeed the change is even more recent and really some would say only started as recently as the 1980's with a woman Prime Minister, the late Baroness Thatcher showed and told women that 'they can' and changed culture not only in the UK but globally. A time when women started to compete for top jobs and leave the selection of pinafore dresses in the wardrobe and aprons on a hook on the back of the kitchen door to gather dust. Microwave platters replaced dinner on the table for the once sole breadwinner and only after he collected the children from the child minder.

Is this why the children of the 80's era are now raising their own kids with only a trace the ideals that their own parents were brought up on in the middle of the last century?

Mothers that used to be homemakers were all of a sudden working too and the work experience generated opinion and thus debate at home and what men identified as 'nagging'. Is this why there are very few books on the subject pre 1980? But once again I digress and look for sociological answers to reinforce the reason why small boys brag and lie in an attempt to sound more important than they really are. These answers will not however make any difference to why boys brag and talk jibberish from an early age.

What is abundantly clear is that if a small boy sees dad, as a role model, then the chances are that he will copy dad's appearance, manner and habits. If, let's say, dad sits on his arse drinking from a can of lager bellowing instructions to his spouse and arguing the toss on doing anything in the house, then it stands a real chance that 'Tyler' will grow up doing the same, telling his mum off and shouting the odds too as he sits on his arse as well, drinking Shandy Bass, pinched from the larder. Father and son might even wear the same muscle top or football shirt and have the same haircut and left ear pierced. Stereotyping, yes but it is there for all to see on the train, bus or plane. These family set up's make great TV which is likely the reason why we see so many 'real life' programmes about Super Nanny, a person drafted in to try and solve behaviour problems with a nine year old child who head butts his mother and sisters instead of kissing them all goodnight and retiring at 8pm for a good nights sleep. In these programmes it is more often a shitty little boy who is the problem, not often a naughty unruly girl. By the end of the programme the analyst's identify the root of the problem by looking no further than the father.

Other programmes might look at posh little boys who follow pater's lead and have an arrogance that is just as annoying as the head butt hooligan mentioned above. More disturbing is how some small boys are made and dressed as mere clones of the father. If papa wears a cravat they may choose or be encouraged to wear cravats too, three boys looking 'damn smart, what' all confident in their own right with opinions and vocabulary beyond their years so that they can engage in conversation with adults. More likely encouraged, by insatiable parents, to show off and exploit their talent for everything they do, and entertain the normal side of the family with the very good family band playing at social gatherings. God help them all though, growing up as Little Lord Fauntleroy's!

Instead of feeling sorry for these kids viewers feel the urge to punch the screen, cocky little baskets!

These are both ends of the spectrum and normal kids will grow into normal adults in good time. What is normal though? It depends who you speak to and what they believe is normal. What is usual is that boys continue to try and impress friends and surpress threats. How difficult is it growing up?

But enough of the serious bit let us move on to teenage boys and the crap they come out with.

Is this and eye opener for the female readers, or a

reminder for male readers? Either way it is observation again gleaned from years or people watching.

Testosterone & Teenagers

A good idea for any parent of a teenage boy is to have unlimited access to a 'bullshit detector'. This wonderful tool however is probably not needed as most cute parents can see through any teenager straight away and recognise a bit of twisted truth before sniggering out loud at the audacity of the comment. This snigger generates another trait in the teenager, the inability to avoid a rush of blood to the face and a glance to the side, which confirms the presence of a bit of bully.

Whether the need to appear manly starts with a surge in testosterone during the pubescent years or whether it starts earlier is irrelevant. The fact remains that boys compare themselves to others from an early age. From the days in the changing rooms and the poor kid that has an acorn for a 'willy' compared to the one with a fifth limb, or the presence of genital hair by an advanced eleven year old, instead of a bald patch that looks like his Action Man, boys yearn to grow up quickly and have a deep voice instead of the squeaky high pitched one. After all, a deep voice means serious man presence; which is why some boys put on a deeper voice before forgetting it is a cover up and revert to their actual voice, an octave or two higher. It is hilarious to their friends and another reason to blush, for the kid that is caught out putting the 'manly' voice.

With puberty come, for want of a better word, more self-awareness and a touch of embarrassment, especially when the innocuous 'lob on' changes from a normal occurrence and a built in toy for a little boy into a hugely, or maybe not that big, embarrassing and uncontrollable situation with a 'pole' that has to be hidden at all costs. If mum walks in to the bedroom to peel back the curtains and drag off the duvet after shouting instructions to "get up" for the last twenty minutes, the horror for a teenager that she will see his morning salute protruding through his Toy Story pyjamas is somewhat mortifying. The solution is to twist over to his front and risk breaking 'it' off in the process, dangerous, very dangerous!

Coupled to the change with his dangly bits come, sorry that word again, the realisation that pee isn't the only thing that can be syphoned from the built in toy. Teenagers think they are being smart, but every parent knows that when cleaning up a teenager's room and picking up discarded underwear, it should always be done with caution. Whether a teenage boy likes it or not socks are only meant to be used to keep feet warm and not as a receptacle for, well I will let you decide of what!

Boys have gone through the stage where girls were equals in the kindergarten and they mixed freely over a box of Lego, even the dress-up box, then comes the horrible stage pulling pigtails and bullying girls because girls are 'yuk'. With testosterone comes an awkward stage where the natural urge is to be cool and attract female attention to boost the ego. These efforts employ saying stupid statements that make a lad sound like a complete retard.

Caught in between wanting to be nice to actually get the attentions they crave and being cool in front of the immature group to avoid heckling and being labelled a 'girl lover' young teenage boys just end up insecure and desperate and revert to bragging to boost self-esteem.

When a lad moves into this phase, he forgets what

a nasty and cruel dick he was for years and even if he always tried to be nice there will definitely be one or two occasions when he was goaded by his deep voiced friends to be mean to a girl. This is where he finally realises that women never forget!

Therefore to get to the manly bit he develops more bullshit to 'impress' girls, but it normally comes out all wrong. This leads on nicely to a bit of bragging that teenage boys partake in when a girl asks questions like these...

I thought you were going out with Sarah?

"Yeh, well I was but we didn't get on so I binned her!"
The truth of the matter is that he probably tried to get his grubby mitts into an area of 'restricted access' and Sarah decided to kick him into touch. Will he ever admit he was chucked, hell no!

This eagerness to 'get off with a girl' or at least to get from first base to second and third bases is so that he can brag to his friends that he has done the deed. Ridiculous but unlocking the achievement is just as important as clearing a difficult level on one of his X-Box games, if not a fair comparison. This is why lads try, fail, try again and use deeper voices to convince girls to put out.

I really hope those that will inevitably try it with my daughter realise that I have a well-oiled baseball bat ready and waiting! What I am sure of though is that she will one day get her own back on any lad that goes too far and god help him when she does!

Leading on from these multiple attempts in teenage years more bullshit is said to his friends and the level of bragging increases to maintain the charade. Lies and false truths litter the conversations between lads.

Did you do it?

"Yes course I did, I was great!"

Probably a lie but failing to make out is far too embar-rassing, so lie and hope that his inquisitive friends don't question the girl involved. Net result is that loads of girls and boys have no idea who has or who hasn't and the league tables are fabricated. But who cares anyway? They all do!

Now, it might be the truth and the two may have actually done it but even if they did to think it was great is another bit of bully. Probably a quick fumble, two strokes and more red faces, all round.

The next bit of bragging is the all too important numbers game, referred to in the first book, and quite honestly the biggest lie that any man will say, all because numbers evidently represent a higher ranking in the manhood stakes. What a load of rubbish!

Seemingly teenagers and adolescents think that more sexual partners equates to a stud factor rating. Bizarrely on the other hand a girl who professes to a similar number is portrayed as a 'slag' so why is it any different for a 'man slag'? Because lads and men encourage each other to chalk another one up on the board..."go on my son!"

How many is that now?

"Oh, losing count, fifty or sixty at least!"

Divide it by three and then square root the answer for an accurate number, if it matters at all. Here's the thing men actually boast to having more than ten in their lifetime whereas the average is nine, according to a health survey by the NHS in 2011; the disturbing fact is that the average for women was four. So how the hell have men sleep with twice as many women if women have slept with half the number of men?

The math doesn't equate. UNLESS there is bullshit factor in the answers, from the men, taken as the true answers, by the researchers.

Reading this, I bet that men will be comparing the average of nine and women the average of four and further comparing their own true number. Do you need to borrow someone else's hands or is one of your own hands enough? Oh, and by the way hand ones don't count if you are using one hand. Whatever, it doesn't mean anything; in fact if anything it only reinforces the ridiculous importance that teenagers and adults put on the 'numbers game' and how the 'bullshit alert' is probably right when teenagers compare notes!

Adolescent Bull

The bullshit isn't reserved for sexual conquests alone, oh no it transfers to material items and excuses for not doing something as well. Have you ever called 'bull' on a comment that a young man says about why he hasn't changed his car, when he said he was; why he didn't go out or turn up to an event when he said he would, or why he hasn't moved out of his parents home when he was going on about a new luxury pad six months ago? There is always an excuse and one explained in detail with the famous "yeh well" inserted at the beginning of the sentence.

If you don't recognise these outward displays of bullshit then a perfect place to hear them is at the sauna and steam rooms at the gym. There are always a couple of 20 something year old blokes that frequent the steam room and speak loudly enough, for all to hear, in fluent bullcrap, while the rest of us are there to chill. Do they not realise that we don't give a shit about why they bought a Subaru and how they pulled a model. Even more hilarious when they are spotted twenty minutes later driving off in a Citroen Saxo!

The same gobshite will still be waffling on in the sauna a month later with the same bragging, and adopts a rather pleasant vocabulary saying, "yeh man. I'm getting a sweet ride next week" now being fluent in young speak this refers to the car he is still going on about, not a gullible woman he hopes to bed.

Another strange thing that I have noticed is the accent, which is a hybrid London twang with a hint of Jamaican even though the orator is white and from Birmingham. What is that all about? When spoken with mannerisms that include alternate shoulders dipping in time to every word and indeed using an alternative pronunciation of the words 'asked' and 'ride', for example "I was like, AKSING her if she liked my RAAYYD" it gets even more intriguing to the spectators sitting in the hot room. Who the hell is this clown and why doesn't he speak in a Brummie accent, in fact why is his friend speaking in the same voice, who are these two clowns?

These stories often refer to 'Cougar Conquests', which appear to be challenges for many a 20 year old. For god's sake, be careful lads, very dangerous ground!

This age coincides with the previous reference in Chapter One to being 'raw meat' for girls of the same age, which is why a lot of lads in their late teens and early twenties end up going out with younger women, seventeen and eighteen year olds who actually fall for the flannel. It is only a little later that the age difference narrows and men end up with someone of a similar age. The excuses carry on into the more mature years. I use the label mature loosely however as men rarely grow up and recognise the waste of energy that bullshitting actually is.

Forty Up

After a life of bragging and half-truths, some may say to keep the peace at home; there is an epiphany for a man that they have had more than enough of having to remember everything to remain a good bullshitter.

To be good at bullshit a man has to be excellent at remembering what they said and to who otherwise they will be caught out by the cross-examination from not only women but also friends and work colleagues.

How many people do you know that have tripped up at some stage when a subject is raised again and they say something completely different? I know that I have caught many people out, especially at work when an excuse was used that miraculously changes to a different excuse a month later. Tempting, as it was to uncover a pile of bullshit, I, like many of us, have more often resisted the temptation and decided that future statements from that person should be taken with a pinch of salt. Telling the truth and owning up to mistakes is far easier and avoids note taking and the need for impulse excuses. Or am I clearly being too rational? Probably!

The funny thing is that being honest is perceived as lying, why? Because for years women are fed excuses and fabricated stories and thus from past experience the common decision is that all men probably always have something to hide from women. The reality is that they are probably right due to the simple fact that men will offer part explanation that is never enough to placate the curious mind of a woman. Oh the joys!

So here we are, a bit of a character assassination of the male of the species and, as with the rest of the book, it doesn't mean that every man is a compulsive liar, the same as every woman isn't a ferocious nagger. Every day a wee comment might come out of a man or a woman's mouth and that might be all for the day or another week. The rest of the time harmony reigns and everyone is happy. Writing a book on the joys of a relationship would be nowhere near as funny as what I have attempted to do in this book or the first offering, would it?

Sorry, fellow men, for adding to the potential for 'nagging', but the female audience requested the alternative view and at my time of life I have all but realised that 'nagging' will never go away and much of it is brought on by us men, reacting a certain way or saying the wrong thing that only fuels the fire. The important part of this Chapter and the rest of the book is that although 'nagging' can be soul destroying, there is always something funny to extract from the comments, clichés and testing questions.

Keep that in mind and there will always be light at the end of the tunnel.

Live and let live!

Si prohibere iugiter, forsitan magis
(If you stopped nagging, perhaps I would do more)

Suggested further reading

"Life of Pie – Nag Pie
(Fifty More Shades of Nagging)
by Chris Gibson

The follow up satirical offering to the hit eBook and paperback 'Fifty Shades of Nagging' that this time discussed the development of a woman in the art of nagging in a journey through life, a "Life of Pie Nag Pie".

Published by alliebooks.co.uk available as an eBook by Original eBooks and Original Writing (UK) Limited available from Amazon, iTunes and all good sites
Bulk order paperback copies are available from the publisher and via Createspace, global distributor.
Parent ISBN 978-1-909429-06-2
ePub version 978-1-909429-07-9
Mobi version 978-1-909429-08-6

"Fifty Shades of Nagging – Most of them Grey!
by Chris Gibson

The first short book penned by Chris Gibson that looked at what couples say to each other in a vague attempt to communicate. Very much a tongue in cheek satirical view written to raise a smile, not over analyse the subject of perceived 'nagging'. Fifty, or so, pages long it is a quick read with over fifty clichés and comments that some might call 'nagging' while others might simply call it 'motivation.'

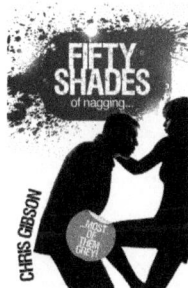

Published by alliebooks.co.uk available as an eBook by Original eBooks and Original Writing (UK) Limited available from Amazon, iTunes and all good sites
Bulk order paperback copies are available from the publisher and via Createspace, global distributor.
Parent ISBN 978-1-909429-00-0
ePub version 978-1-909429-02-4
Mobi version 978-1-909429-01-7

"Golf Speak Exposed - The Crazy Things That Golfers Say!

by Chris Gibson

The third funny book penned by Chris Gibson that looks at what millions of golfers say on courses all over the world to excuse poor shots and offer an explanation or commentary to playing partners. A collection of cliches and over used phrases with some alternative answers that could be said in reply, save the need for etiquette that the great game dictates! (print length 88 pages)

Published by alliebooks.co.uk available as an eBook by Original eBooks and Original Writing (UK) Limited available from Amazon, iTunes and all good sites
Bulk order paperback copies are available from the publisher and via Createspace, global distributor.
Parent ISBN 978-1-909429-09-3
ePub version 978-1-909429-10-9
Mobi version 978-1-909429-11-6

(Business books by the author)

**"Franchising Exposed – A Definitive Guide
for anyone looking to buy a franchise or develop
a franchise concept"
by Chris Gibson**
Chris Gibson's first book first published in 2011 and
written to help people looking to start a new business
or convert an existing business into a licensed
franchise partnership. Advice and anecdotes that can
help make the right informed decision

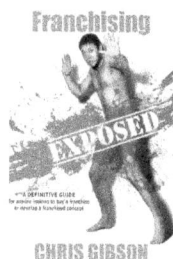

*Published by alliebooks.co.uk available as an eBook by Original eBooks and Original
Writing (UK) Limited available from Amazon, iTunes and all good sites*
*Bulk order paperback copies are available from the publisher and via Createspace,
global distributor.*
Parent ISBN 978-0-9567618-0-4 (paperback 2011)
ePub version 978-0-9567618-8-0
Mobi version 978-0-9567618-9-7

**"Selling, it's not a Mind Trick"
by Chris Gibson & Alan Guinn**
First published in 2012 and written with co-author
Alan Guinn, a veteran of training people all over the
world via selling seminars. Collectively this book is
a combination of over 70 years experience in sales
and selling with tip and advice that are designed to
help sales executives and the CEO alike.

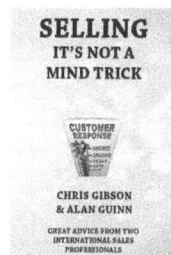

*Published by alliebooks.co.uk available as an eBook by Original eBooks and Original
Writing (UK) Limited available from Amazon, iTunes and all good sites*
Bulk order paperback copies are available from the publisher and via Createspace,
global distributor.
Parent ISBN 978-0-9567618-5-9
ePub version 978-0-9567618-6-6
Mobi version 978-0-9567618-7-3

"Selling Skills Exposed – Brilliant Sales Techniques"
by Chris Gibson
& Alan Guinn

A revised look at 'Selling, it's not a Mind Trick' published in 2013, with a new 'search friendly' title and to coincide with global availability on Amazon.

Published by alliebooks.co.uk available as an eBook by Original eBooks and Original Writing (UK) Limited available from Amazon, iTunes and all good sites
Bulk order paperback copies are available from the publisher and via Createspace, global distributor.
Parent ISBN 978-1-909429-03-1
ePub version 978-1-909429-04-8
Mobi version 978-1-909429-05-5

"So...You Want to Buy a Franchise"
by Alan Guinn & Chris Gibson

Written for the US market, although it translates to any language this is essential reading for anyone looking to enter the wonderful world of franchising and start a business. Advice on business planning, operation and sales techniques are also included.

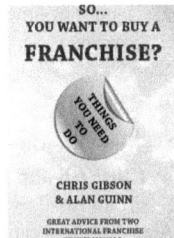

Published by alliebooks.co.uk available as an eBook by Original eBooks and Original Writing (UK) Limited available from Amazon, iTunes and all good sites
Bulk order paperback copies are available from the publisher and via Createspace, global distributor.
Parent ISBN 978-0-9567618-4-8
ePub version 978-0-9567618-3-5
Mobi version 978-0-9567618-2-8

"Psyched for Life – A New Guide to Decision Making"
by Alan Guinn

First published in 2001, a short book written by Alan Guinn to focus the reader on how to make effective decisions and avoid procrastination.

Published by Alan Guinn available from Amazon
ISBN 978-0-9712707-0-1

www.ingramcontent.com/pod-product-compliance
Lightning Source LLC
Chambersburg PA
CBHW061726020426
42331CB00006B/1114